Poemas Humanos
Human Poems

Poemas Humanos

Human Poems

by César Vallejo

Translated by Clayton Eshleman

Grove Press, Inc., New York

Editor's Note: The dates that appear in brackets after certain of the poems are estimated dates of composition. Those dates that are unbracketed are, as far as can be determined, the dates Vallejo put to each poem upon its completion:

The Spanish text was originally published in Paris, France, in 1939 by Les Éditions des Presses Modernes au Palais-Royal as *Poemas Humanos*.

Many of these translations, in their present or earlier versions, have appeared in the following periodicals: *Burning Water, Camels Coming, Caterpillar, Caw!, Choice, Contemporary Literature in Translation, East Village Other, El Corno Emplumado, Evergreen Review, Folio, Kulchur, Maps, The Nation, Origin (second series), Potpourri, Prairie Schooner, Quark, Tish, Tri-Quarterly*.

First Evergreen Edition, 1969
Second Printing

Manufactured in the United States of America

DISTRIBUTED BY RANDOM HOUSE, INC., NEW YORK

Translator's Foreword

1. Biographical Information

On April 15, 1938, having swept down the Ebro valley, the Spanish Nationalists reached the Mediterranean. In the film *To Die in Madrid* there is a scene of the troops frolicking in the surf. On the same day, at dawn, one of the greatest poets of the modern era cried out in delirium from his deathbed in a Parisian clinic, "I am going to Spain! I want to go to Spain!"

César Abraham Vallejo was born in the medieval Andean town of Santiago de Chuco, in northern Peru, on March 16, 1892. The youngest of eleven children, César grew up in a home saturated in religious devotion; his family openly hoped he would become a priest. Juan Larrea and Juan Espejo, friends and biographers of the poet, speak of the profound anguish in Vallejo caused by the conflict between the spiritual and the worldly – especially in regard to his erotic experiences – which had its roots in the deep idealism, the sense of sin, good, and evil, of such Catholic upbringing.

When he was eighteen, Vallejo went to Trujillo for the first time and enrolled in the university as a student in *Letras.* He soon ran out of money and went to work in the mining town of Quiruvilca. A year later, with family aid, he again tried the university, this time in Lima. It turned out that his family could not support him, and 1911 and 1912 find him working as a tutor for the owner's children in a sierra hacienda. With savings, he entered the university at Trujillo in 1913 and received his Bachelor's degree two years later. It was on the hacienda that Vallejo, whose grandmothers were pure Indian,

saw Indians flogged and working for a few cents a day, and in Quiruvilca that he found inspiration for his novel, *El Tungsteno*, written in 1931. The major development in his life, that of the emergence of the engaged European Communist from the expatriate Peruvian poet, may well have turned on what he saw and felt years before.

One of Vallejo's hacienda roommates relates that on Sunday, their only day off, Vallejo would go for walks and read instead of getting drunk with the other employees, and that often he would show this roommate his first attempts at poetry. It was during his university days in Trujillo, however, that he really began to read and was introduced by Antenor Orrego, a journalist and the local intellectual guide, to others his own age, some of whom were to become nationally famous in literature, journalism, and politics. Orrego, who was then working on the newspaper *La Reforma*, recalls: "Along about November or December of 1914 Vallejo approached me bringing a notebook of poems. I can't remember how many, certainly no more than twenty-five or thirty poems. It was then I became aware of all the reading he was doing on his own, of all Spanish literature from the Golden Age on, and that his poetic imitations went back as far as Gonzalo de Berceo. There were magnificent imitations of Quevedo as well as Lope, Tirso and many others." During his student years, Vallejo supported himself teaching grade school part-time in Trujillo; in later years, no matter how complex and impassioned his thought became, it was often conveyed through a grade-school teacher's knowledge of the human body, mathematics, and grammar.

By 1916 Vallejo was regularly publishing poetry in Orrego's *La Reforma*, poetry that was later printed in his first book, *Los Heraldos Negros*. He was reading Emerson, Unamuno, Darío, Nervo, Herrera y Reissig and, in translation, the French Symbolists. He managed to get himself attacked by conservative Trujillan society for satirizing them in a sonnet, and throughout 1916 and 1917 he was tied up in anguished love affairs. A photo taken at this time shows Vallejo's high Indian cheekbones and heavy black hair — a very handsome face.

In 1918 he went to Lima and became known to some distinguished men of letters, one of whom, Abraham Valdelomar,

agreed to write the prologue to his first book. He continued to teach grade school. When *Los Heraldos Negros* appeared in the summer of 1919 it was received politely and somewhat enthusiastically; the impression is that at the time Vallejo had filled to brimming the antiquated forms literary society found acceptable – to continue to push his talent in its own directions would soon bring him hostility and silence.

In 1920, returning home after two years' absence, he passed with a friend through Huamanchuco (where he had attended high school) and visited with his brother. Vallejo and his friend edited a law paper and with their pay went off to a saloon. They came back drunk. Vallejo had been invited that evening to read in his old high school, and after reciting a poem he waited for the applause. When there was none, he became furious with the audience's attitude and said, "Since you don't applaud me, little do I care for your applause now that the intellectuals of the country applaud me. One day my poetry will make me greater than even Rubén Darío – I'll know the pride of seeing America prostrated before my feet." This caused a scandal in town, during which Vallejo rode off for Santiago to attend the annual festival of the patron saint.

He rode into a town feud that had been smoldering since the last elections. On the last Sunday of the festival violence broke out – a deputy was killed and the general store, owned by a family whose political ties were opposed to those of the Vallejo family, was burned to the ground. Vallejo, who was helping the Sub-prefect write the legal information about the killing, was blamed as an accomplice in the burning and later, in court, as the "intellectual instigator." He was found guilty and spent 105 days in a Trujillo jail after which he was forced to live in Trujillo six months. The whole business embittered him terribly.

Before serving his sentence, Vallejo had hidden in a cottage belonging to Orrego; there he began the book that for many critics breaks Latin American poetry out of its nineteenth-century tradition and links it to a twentieth-century European context. In 1922, having submitted a manuscript–to be printed with his own funds–called "Craneos de Bronce" which was to be printed under the name of César Perú, Vallejo was scoffed at by friends who said he was affecting an imitation of

D'Annunzio and Anatole France. He decided to use his own name. Then he was told that the first pages of the book had been printed and a name change would cost him extra, "*tres libras.*" Apparently he didn't have three dollars, for Espejo relates: "Vallejo felt mortified. Several times he repeated *tres, tres, tres,* with that insistence he had for repeating words and deforming them, *tresss, trisss, trieesss, tril, trilssss.* He stammered and in the lisp came out *trilsssce . . . trilce? trilce?* He hesitated for a moment, then exclaimed: 'O.k., I'll use my own name but the book will be called *Trilce.*' "

Trilce contains seventy-seven poems and to anyone who has read Latin American poetry written before it, it is a very strange book indeed – it seems to come out of nowhere. André Coyné, Vallejo's most astute critic, states: "In *Trilce* there is no universe, nor objects, except those furtively introduced across the unadorned and familiar world of the hearth and love; we are presented only with rapid sensations, glimpsed in a semiconscious or semivigilant state, and (now that the eye hardly has a role) received like shocks and indicated solely by a painful resonance always without resolution – a resonance that is internal, visceral. . . . Poems that hardly are poems, traced on the birthlike and insistent talk of childhood or fever, each stanza organizing on the basis of a separate intuition, for the poet is always at the mercy of the sudden attack of this or that term or the pressing in of anxiety."

After the publication of *Trilce,* Vallejo continued to live in Lima. In the spring of 1923 he was notified that his teaching position had been eliminated. At about the same time he was offered a post as the Lima correspondent for a Trujillo newspaper, and when he found that he could fulfill the post in Europe, he made plans to leave. On a June Sunday, with his friend Julio Galvez and a hundred and fifty dollars, he embarked third-class for France. He never returned to Peru.

At this point in César Vallejo's life all biographical continuity ends. The rather sketchy knowledge that we have concerning the European years (1923–1938) is based on information from Georgette de Vallejo, the poet's widow. Thus, it is hoped, the reader can at least get a sense of the poet's full but frustrating life in Europe.

1923 and 1924 seem to have been the years that Vallejo nearly starved in Paris. In 1923, he and Galvez walked the streets looking for bottles to cash in. The next year, the Costa Rican sculptor, Max Jiménez, left them his studio. Vallejo translated a book on Peru into Spanish for 1000 francs. He met the painter Juan Gris, Juan Larrea, and the poet Vicente Huidobro. In 1925, Vallejo found his first stable job with Le Bureau des Grands Journaux Ibero-americains, and began a long collaboration with *Mundial*, a Lima weekly. During this year he made his first trip to Spain where he received a small writer's grant through the Peruvian Embassy in Madrid.

In 1926 he lived in the Hôtel Richelieu in Paris and went to exhibitions, concerts, and cafés, and met Antonin Artaud and Waldo Frank. With Juan Larrea, he co-edited a magazine, *Favorables París Poema*, which published contributions by Huidobro, Neruda, Reverdy, Tzara, and Gris. He became a weekly columnist for *Variedades*, published in Lima, and an essay of his, *Poesía Nueva*, published in *Amauta*, introduced French Surrealist poets to Peruvian readers. In 1927, in the first of a number of political gestures, he left his post at Le Bureau, and an essay, *Contra el secreto Profesional*, appeared in *Variedades*. In this essay Vallejo discussed the double failure of South American poets to use European influences and to find an expression indigenous to their own people. At this period the idea that lay under all of Vallejo's journalism was the conviction that poetry must become a direct language, freed from traditional devices.

In 1928 he read much Marxist literature, and attended lectures on dialectical materialism, living off odd jobs. He lived, for the summer, in the town of Ris-Oranges, and in September left for Russia. He returned in November and began living with Georgette Philippart. In December, along with Mariátegui, he broke with the Peruvian revolutionary movement, APRA, in which they detected a fascist base. The next year, 1929, his Marxist studies continuing, he taught in worker cells and decided to publish no more poetry in the belief that the artist's role was, for the time being, economic. In September he again journeyed to Russia where, in Moscow, he interviewed Mayakovsky. On his way back to Paris he traveled through Berlin,

Vienna, Florence, Rome, and Nice. That November he worked on a notebook of meditations on Marxist theory and its application to the Soviet Union: he was now committed to Communism.

Early in 1930, a Madrid magazine, *Bolívar*, carried a piece of his reportage on Russia, later to be incorporated into *Rusia en 1931*. He wrote his first drama, *Mampar*. In May he and Mme Vallejo traveled to Spain where he met such writers as Salinas, Alberti, Unamuno, and Gerardo Diego. The critic José Bergamín wrote an introduction to the second edition of *Trilce* (which appeared in July). Pierre Lagarde, writing of the volume, said: "Vallejo has invented Surrealism before the surrealists." In June the couple returned to Paris and Vallejo began his second play, *Moscú contra Moscú*. The weekly meetings that he attended in L'Humanité book shop were watched by the police and in December Vallejo was ordered to leave France in three days. Again, he returned to Spain.

In 1931, in Madrid, he wrote the novel, *El Tungsteno*, and translated novels by Marcel Aymé and Henri Barbusse. The Monarchy had just fallen and the Republic proclaimed. It was now that Vallejo officially joined the Communist party and became one of the founders of Spanish Communist cells. For the first time in his life, he was well received in important literary circles, and frequently met with Bergamín, Alberti, and Lorca. La Editorial Ulises published *Rusia en 1931* in July, and a second and third edition followed shortly. In Moscow a literary conference was organized, based on the book; Vallejo was temporarily famous. In October he traveled in Russia and took part in the International Congress of Authors in Moscow. He arrived back in Madrid penniless, and with a notebook which eventually became *Rusia ante el Segundo Plan Quinquenal*. He wrote another play, *Lockout*, and the story, "Paco Yunque." Notwithstanding his relative success with the Russian travel book, he could not find a publisher for his plays or stories.

Mme Vallejo returned to Paris in January, 1932, to arrange for Vallejo's return and found their apartment ransacked by the police. The poet stayed at a pension in Madrid. Within the space of a month he submitted his collection of essays, *El Arte y La Revolución*, to a publisher, and it was refused; he sub-

mitted *Moscú contra Moscú* and *Lockout*, and they were refused; Lorca offered to read *Mampar* at the Cervantes Theater, but before the reading, the theater closed; Vallejo offered *Rusia ante el Segundo Plan Quinquenal*, still in progress, to two publishers, and it was refused; Lorca read *Moscú contra Moscú* to a producer who told him it was unpresentable, and Lorca proposed to read it to another producer. But Vallejo wanted to get back to Paris, and on hearing that a resident permit had been obtained, arrived there in February with nothing but the clothes he was wearing.

In 1933, he and Mme Vallejo were living in the Hôtel Garibaldi, and Vallejo was revising poems. He also worked on more plays, compiled a second volume of studies and essays, *Contra el secreto Profesional*, and published, in *Germinal*, a seven-part article, *¿Qué pasa en el Perú?*. He wrote, in 1934, a satire of Peruvian political life, *Los Hermanos Colacho*. His precarious financial situation and bad luck continued throughout 1935, and the couple took a room on the Boulevard Raspail, while Vallejo searched for work.

1936 found Vallejo teaching Spanish. He published *El hombre y Dios en la escultura incaica* in *Beaux-Arts*. He and Mme Vallejo moved here and there, finally settling in the Hôtel du Maine. The Fascist uprising in Spain in July stirred him to a flurry of activity. He attended meetings and assemblies in Paris, canvassed the streets to collect money, and at night waited in Montparnasse station for telegrams from Madrid. He soon left for Spain, extremely upset, and traveled to Barcelona and Madrid. At the end of December he returned to Paris, completely absorbed in the Spanish cause.

In 1937 he founded, with others, the Comité Ibero-americana para la defensa de la República Española, and its publicity bulletin, "Nuestra España." To raise money he wrote a film script, *Charlot contra Chaplin*. He left again in July for Spain, which by now was deep in civil war, and took part in the Segundo Congreso Internacional de Escritores para la defensa de la Cultura which met in Valencia, Madrid, and Barcelona, and closed in Paris. On this final return from Spain, the dam broke: Vallejo wrote *La Piedra Cansada*, a fifteen-scene tragedy, and then, after nearly fifteen years of poetic silence, turned all his energy toward revising, finishing, and writing the poems that

were to eventually make up *Poemas Humanos*. This tremendous labor of writing the drama and the majority of the ninety-four poems of *Poemas Humanos* took place roughly between August and early December. Either during this time or just after, he wrote a sheaf of fifteen poems inspired by the Republican cause, *España, aparte de mí este Cáliz*, which was printed by Republican soldiers. The entire edition was lost in the disaster of Cataluña.

The years of strain and deprivation, psychic illness over the fall of the Republic, and exhaustion from the pace of the previous year, finally, in 1938, took their toll. In March Vallejo was in bed with a constant fever. X rays and analysis showed no cause for alarm, but he could not get out of bed and his fever persisted. The Peruvian Embassy had him moved to the Arago clinic where, despite medical attention, his condition steadily worsened. On March 29, he dictated to Mme Vallejo: "Whatever may be the cause I have to defend before God, beyond death I have a defender: God." On April 14, he lost consciousness, medical analysis still having shown no cause for his illness. The hospital records stated that his death, at 9:30 A.M., Good Friday, April 15, was the effect of an acute intestinal infection, but friends and other authorities have claimed that the cause of death was never determined. His body was buried on April 19, in Montrouge cemetery.

In 1939 his widow brought out *Poemas Humanos* in a limited edition. In 1940, the Spanish Civil War sheaf was published. As incredible as it may seem, much of the rest of Vallejo's writing – which as far I can judge comes to four full-length dramas, two novels, two volumes of essays, a film script, a half-dozen notebooks, and a volume of miscellaneous prose – remains in manuscript.[1]

[1] This situation was partially remedied with the 1967 publication of *Novelas y Cuentos Completos* by Francisco Moncloa Editores, Lima, Peru. This volume contains the collection of short stories, *Escalas Melografiadas*; the novels, *El Tungsteno* and *Hacia el reino de los Sciris*; the novella, *Fabla Salvaje*; the short story, "Paco Yunque"; and the fragment of a novel, *Sabiduría*. There are also included four previously unpublished stories. In 1965, there was also published in Lima his second book on Russia, *Rusia ante el Segundo Plan Quinquenal*.

2. *César Vallejo: Black Stone on a White Stone*

César Vallejo in black overcoat leans, or rests, against a lichen-mottled boulder, mostly white, or suggesting that contrast in Juan Larrea's photo, 1926, Paris, bosque de Fontainebleau. He appears to be in meditation – the darkness where are the eyes suggests a death mask – the head is starved – hair too high and feeling too airy and brushed back to be sensual. His shoes and socks suggest foreign students – he is at home mostly symbolically. He died in 1938, in Paris, and the actual death mask is pitted and full fleshed.

It is difficult to know enough about Vallejo. Most of his writings, as previously noted, are not available in any language. His widow, Georgette Vallejo, who has lived for many years in Lima on a pension given her by the Peruvian government, holds much of his writing – which includes critical essays, drama (influenced by Antonin Artaud and studied by García Lorca), journals, a novel, and probably more poetry than the four published volumes which are said to constitute the *obra poetica.*[2] There is also a great deal – 200 articles at least – of journalism buried in the archives of the Peruvian National Library, most of which Vallejo wrote while in Europe and mailed back to Peruvian weeklies. This journalism constitutes an intellectual biography and I have read very little of it. The entire biography, or *vida,* is cloaked in mystery.

Vallejo speaks very naturally in the tone and compassion of Jesus in *Poemas Humanos*; there is almost nothing literary about his Christianity – he lived it, dreadfully, died on Good Friday and a few months before his death called his last sheaf of poems *Spain, let this Cup pass from Me.* There is no satis-

[2] For example, in the second volume of her *Diary* Anaïs Nin remarks: "Gonzalo thinks about death. 'And suddenly the heart stops beating.' He tells me how Vallejo never showed his poetry, that he had tons and tons of it all over his room that nobody had ever read. And that he told in one poem, how he would die on All Saints' Day, and then that day came and he did die." (Anaïs Nin, *The Diary of Anaïs Nin, Volume 2, 1935–1939.* New York: Harcourt, Brace & World, 1967.)

Gonzalo is Gonzalo More, another Peruvian, and one of Vallejo's best friends.

factory explanation of his death. One of his critics, Xavier Abril, reproduces a photo of the death certificate that states death was due to an "acute intestinal infection." Mme Vallejo claims this is false information, and that Vallejo died from a reoccurring case of malaria. There is no evidence I know of concerning this. At the end of his essay,[3] H. R. Hays notes: "In the larger sense he was struck down by hunger and by Spain's agony." There is certainly truth in these words: "The Starving Man's Rack," written during the first years Vallejo lived in Paris, records a hunger that while physical is spiritual to the extent that it could, and most probably did, damage the poet's body. Vallejo's sickness often seems rooted in his stomach, to arise from the matrix of his being, a "slip-up" as he calls it, in the very framework of things. This framework was also social; Vallejo believed in the Russian Revolution to such an extent that when he extended his belief to Spain and then saw that belief crumble in the mid-thirties (in 1937 he spent a month traveling in Spain from city to city while the country was literally convulsing in flames), something collapsed in his own constitution – Spain's *agon* became his own in the *España* sheaf, and too in this book, completed probably before the Spanish Civil War poems were done – or, I should guess, overlapped with them. But in *Poemas Humanos* this struggle is interiorized and then projected to all men, in Vallejo's own person, as contradiction and violence therein. Only one of *Poemas Humanos* is overtly political, "Angelic Greeting," written in the early thirties at the height of his Marxist conversion. Even then he was not much off his own center: he believes and doesn't believe; revolution, he says, through its violent means of betrayal is and is not a solution; perhaps it is the best non-solution. For in Vallejo there is no solution other than death, as "solution" dissolving all. All other solutions as such fade, in *Poemas Humanos*, before all-powerful death; it is as if man never dies but lives eternally at the edge of death. Vallejo is the great poet of the End and in this respect he reminds one of Baudelaire – he is filled with it, an anguish, a Black Midas.

---

[3] H. R. Hays, "The Passion of César Vallejo," *New Directions Annual*, Number 15, 1955.

I felt at first that Vallejo's words could be improved on in English – the first three versions of *Human Poems* are shot through with arbitrary words and line breaks. This was Vallejo's failure to budge. What I bit at, at teeth. He, in contrast to someone like Neruda, would not allow himself to be played with unless he was fingered with devotion – as in the case of Blake, the poem had been written selflessly; while Vallejo and Neruda had crossed at the juncture of the South American Surreal (Vallejo: *Trilce*; Neruda: *Residencia en la Tierra*, I), Neruda found in the third book of *Residencia* the key to becoming *the* twentieth-century South American Poet: the revolutionary stance which always changes with the tides of time. With that recognition and its acceptance Neruda became a figure – or let us say his detachment worked. Vallejo, in spite of his travels from country to country, never could come to terms with one system, and it seems to be to his benefit, for he has produced a poetry dense in texture that holds his feelings and, in reading, releases them.

I translated and lived with Neruda's poetry for a couple of years before encountering Vallejo, and I would like to make this point: that in Vallejo, and *not* in Neruda, the entire consciousness of modern South American man is suffered and partially redeemed; Neruda stays within the bounds of what we (North Americans and Europeans) have expected from South America – the anaconda in the Brazilian swamp, *contra Yanqui*, gorgeous and metrical; the *Poemas Humanos* of Vallejo are still in South America *not* read, because the consciousness is *altered*. Vallejo attacks at root the Catholic-racist-colonial culture that many of the best in South America are still in the nets of. *In Vallejo the amount of physical suffering is the alteration that it seeks*; he poses the problem for the poets who follow him even more crucially than Blake: given the fact that man suffers and that I, as a poet, am always responsible for his suffering, what can I do to lessen this suffering – *as a poet*? Is there a point at which the true poet is no longer a literary man but resumes his place as primal Adam? At the end of *Jerusalem* Blake overthrows all outward ceremony and envisions the apocalypse in self-sacrifice and forgiveness; the poetic act becomes the human act – I forgive you! said with all the heart is greater than *writing* the poem –

it *is* the poem; Vallejo's sickness is not a matter of literary concern – it leads directly to Wilhelm Reich. This Peruvian, revealing the rack in the foundation of his armature, tells us: You must get well.

So was I charged. Utter enlightenment working out over the years. I asked others to read each draft – or strata, as I now call them – of the work. The deeper I went the more literally I worked – I hope I have made a good literal version of *Poemas Humanos*. Nothing to despise about that word. Better, I decided, at about the fifth stratum, to stick with what is awkward at times when it is written by a man trying very hard not to deceive himself. Zukofsky's work on Catullus gave me a certain courage to try out unusual constructions: the crispness and precision of Cid Corman's handling of Montale and Basho gave me a sound-texture to strike at. Thank you Allen, thank you Cid, thank you Louis, thank you Rafael, thank you Claudia, thank you Sidney, thank you Olga, thank you Octavio, thank you Margaret, thank you Vinholes, thank you Maureen – Maureen Maurer – who has spent two years with this manuscript, checking it with me and even more importantly checking it with Mme Vallejo, some of whose suggestions have been incorporated into the final draft; and thank you Mme Vallejo.

At this point some textual details should be mentioned. *Poemas Humanos* was published in an edition of 250 copies in Paris by Georgette Vallejo the year after Vallejo's death, and from her viewpoint is all the poetry he wrote (along with the Spanish Civil War sheaf of fifteen poems) in Europe. Apparently Vallejo intended a collection of poems to be called *Poemas Humanos* and suggested this as a title to his wife some time before his death. The poems that make up the manuscript were left in work sheets, and were copied for publication by Mme Vallejo; thus there are words and punctuation that are her guesses. It is exceedingly difficult to determine how accurate the Spanish text is because no editor or translator has yet had access to the originals. This basic problem is made even more complicated by the fact that printing errors made in the first edition were copied in subsequent editions and new errors were made: some of Vallejo's

intentional misspellings were corrected, periods and commas were left out, stanzas were inverted, and once one poem made of two, and once two poems made of one. I don't think it is necessary here for me to go into all of this since such work is the kind of scholarship that should have been done years ago by South American scholars. Suffice it to say that I used five editions of *Poemas Humanos*, all of which were different, in making my translation, and then in Lima I read these five editions against Mme Vallejo's corrected first edition. Thus the Spanish text in this book seems to me to be the most correct one available anywhere, but there are errors in it that will not be discovered until Vallejo's work sheets can be properly inspected.

The order of the poems in the book is also problematic. It appears that when Mme Vallejo originally copied out the poems for publication she made no attempt to arrange them with any specific order in mind, chronological or poetic. Some of the poems were dated; others were not. She now claims that these dates indicate when a poem was *finished*, not when it was *written*. That is, she would say that a certain poem was written in 1931 and then kept in work sheet until the fall of 1937 when Vallejo for the first time apparently made an effort to make a book, and revised or finished the poem he wrote in 1931. This is not clear at all, but I am recording it here as it was told me. Therefore, since Mme Vallejo did not trust the dates on fifty-two of the poems in the collection, she had them removed in 1958 when a small press, Peru Nuevo, published the book in Peru for the first time. However, the order of the poems in the book remained unchanged and the book ended, as it always had in previous editions, with the longest prose poem, "The windows have been shaken" at the end of which the author presumably dies.[4] The other prose poems in the collec-

[4] Mme Vallejo now says that all the prose poems belong to a separate collection called *Codigo Civil* written between 1923 and 1928, yet she published them as part of *Poemas Humanos* in 1939. They seem to me so much of a piece of the fabric of *Poemas Humanos* that until there is definite evidence that Vallejo intended them to be read in separate format I will consider them part of this volume.

tion were placed right before "The windows . . . ," and it has always appeared that Vallejo wrote the prose poems just before he died. This is not true, nor is it a good idea not to respect Vallejo's ordering of his own life-work, i.e., his dating of poems he obviously considered finished in that gigantic autumn of his poetic consummation in 1937. When I lived in Lima I put all the dates back on the dated poems and one night cut up a copy of the book and put the poems in order. An amazing curve resulted, totally coherent, of a build in intensity through September and October into the half-dozen or so truly magnificent poems written in November. The only poem dated in December is "Sermon on Death" which seems to end that particular production. Therefore I believe the dated poems should be read in their chronological order. Of course a new problem crops up for which a solution can only be suggested in this book: What to do with the poems that have no dates on them? Undoubtedly, these undated poems were, as were many of the dated ones, worked out over a period of years (roughly, I'd say, the bulk of them, between 1931 and 1937). We know through the few available letters of the poet that he was very very sick around the end of 1924 and I am confident that the long "The windows . . ." prose poem refers to this sickness. I have used this piece as a cornerstone to build the other forty-one inexactly dated poems around, and in doing so I have taken into consideration changes in style, and Vallejo's themes. For example, the poems overtly about Peru strike me as being written fairly soon after the poet came to Europe. I am sure I have made some poor guesses and that some of the undated poems belong to the fall 1937 period. However, since such distortion seems minimal, I will elaborate no further. My work is done.

17 January 1968
New York City

Poemas Humanos
Human Poems

Índice

Contents

The Undated Poems [1923 (?)–1937]

The Dated Poems [4 September–8 December, 1937]

The Undated Poems

[1923 (?)–1937]

El Lomo de las Sagradas Escrituras

Sin haberlo advertido jamás exceso por turismo
y sin agencias
de pecho en pecho hacia la madre unánime.

Hasta París ahora vengo a ser hijo. Escucha
Hombre, en verdad te digo que eres el HIJO ETERNO,
pues para ser hermano tus brazos son escasamente iguales
y tu malicia para ser padre, es mucha.

La talla de mi madre, moviéndose por índole de movimiento
y poniéndome serio, me llega exactamente al corazón:
pensando cuanto cayera de vuelo con mis triste abuelos,
mi madre me oye en diámetro, callándose en altura.

Mi metro está midiendo ya dos metros,
mis huesos concuerdan en género y en número
y el verbo encarnado habita entre nosotros
y el verbo encarnado habita al hundirse en el baño,
un alto grado de perfección.

[*Publicado en la revista* Mundial *de Lima, del 11 de noviembre de 1927.*]

Loin of the Scriptures

Without having it ever noted an excess by tourism
and without agencies
from breast to breast toward the unanimous mother.

I'm going to Paris now to be a son. Listen
Man, truthfully I tell you you are the ETERNAL SON,
for to be a brother your arms are hardly equal
and your malice to be a father is tremendous.

My mother's figure, moving according to the nature of movement
and making me serious, hits me right in the heart:
thinking how often she's fallen from flight with my sad grand-
parents
my mother hears me in diameter, silencing on high.

My meter now measures two,
my bones agree in gender and number
and the incarnate word lives among us
and the incarnate word lives sinking in the toilet,
a high degree of perfection.

[*Published in Lima in* Mundial *on November 11, 1927.*]

El Buen Sentido

—Hay, madre, un sitio en el mundo, que se llama París. Un sitio muy grande y lejano y otra vez grande.

Mi madre me ajusta el cuello del abrigo, no por que empieza a nevar, sino para que empiece a nevar.

La mujer de mi padre está enamorada de mí, viniendo y avanzando de espaldas a mi nacimiento y de pecho a mi muerte. Que soy dos veces suyo: por el adiós y por el regreso. La cierro, al retornar. Por eso me dieran tánto sus ojos, justa de mi, infraganti de mí, aconteciéndose por obras terminadas, por pactos consumados.

¿Mi madre está confesa de mí, nombrada de mí? ¿Cómo no da otro tanto a mis otros hermanos? A Víctor, por ejemplo, el mayor, que es tan viejo ya, que las gentes dicen: ¡Parece hermano menor de su padre! ¡Fuere porque yo he viajado mucho! ¡Fuere porque yo he vivido más!

Mi madre acuerda carta de principio colorante a mis relatos de regreso. Ante mi vida de regreso, recordando que viajé durante dos corazones por su vientre, se ruboriza y se queda mortalmente lívida, cuando digo, en el tratado del alma: Aquella noche fuí dichoso. Pero más se pone triste; más se pusiera triste.

Common Sense

—There is, mother, a place in the world, called Paris. A very big place and far off and once again big.

My mother turns up my overcoat collar, not because it is beginning to snow, but so it may.

My father's wife is in love with me, coming and advancing backward toward my birth and breastward toward my death. For I'm hers twice: by the goodbye and by the return. I close her on returning. That's why her eyes gave so much to me, just with me, in flagrante with me, happening by terminated works, by consummated pacts.

My mother is confessed by me, pointed at because of me? How come she doesn't give an equal part to my other brothers? To Victor, for example, the eldest, who is so old now people say: He looks like his father's younger brother! It must be because I've traveled much! Because I've lived more!

My mother grants a map of coloring principle to my stories of return. Facing my life of returning, remembering that I traveled two hearts along her womb, she blushes and stays mortally livid when I say in the treatise of the soul: That night I was happy. But more she becomes sad; more would she become sad.

—Hijo, ¡cómo estás viejo!

Y desfila por el color amarillo a llorar, porque me halla envejecido, en la hoja de espada, en la desembocadura de mi rostro. Llora de mí, se entristece de mí. ¿Qué falta hará mi mocedad, si siempre seré su hijo? ¿Por qué las madres se duelen de hallar envejecidos a sus hijos, si jamás la edad de ellos alcanzará a la de ellas? ¿Y por qué, si los hijos, cuanto más se acaban, más se aproximan a los padres? ¡Mi madre llora porque estoy viejo de mi tiempo y porque nunca llegaré a envejecer del suyo!

Mi adiós partió de un punto de su sér, más externo que el punto de su sér al que retorno. Soy, a causa del excesivo plazo de mi vuelta, más el hombre ante mi madre que el hijo ante mi madre. Allí reside el candor que hoy nos alumbra con tres llamas. Le digo entonces hasta que me callo:

—Hay, madre, en el mundo, un sitio que se llama París. Un sitio muy grande y muy lejano y otra vez grande.

La mujer de mi padre, al oírme, almuerza y sus ojos mortales descienden suavemente por mis brazos.

—You look so old, my son!

And steps along the yellow color to weep, for she finds me aged in the sword blade, in the mouth of my face. Weeps for me, becomes sad for me. How can she miss my youth if I'm always to be her son? Why does a mother ache finding her sons aged, if their ages never reach hers? And why, when the sons the nearer the end they come, the nearer their parents? My mother weeps because I am old in my time and because never will I age in hers!

My goodbye started from a point in her béing, more external than the point in her béing to which I return. I am, because of the excessive deadline of my shift, more man in my mother's eyes than son. There resides the pure whiteness that today sheds light upon us with three flames. I say to her, then, until I hush:

—There is, mother, in the world a place called Paris. A very big place and far off and once again big.

My father's wife, hearing me, eats her lunch and her mortal eyes lower softly by my arms.

Sombrero, Abrigo, Guantes

Enfrente a la Comedia Francesa, está el Café
de la Regencia; en él hay una pieza
recóndita, con una butaca y una mesa.
Cuando entro, el polvo inmóvil se ha puesto ya de pie.

Entre mis labios hechos de jebe, la pavesa
de un cigarrillo humea, y en el humo se ve
dos humos intensivos, el tórax del Café,
y en el tórax, un óxido profundo de tristeza.

Importa que el otoño se injerte en los otoños,
importa que el otoño se integre de retoños,
la nube, de semestres; de pómulos, la arruga.

Importa oler a loco postulando
¡qué cálida es la nieve, qué fugaz la tortuga,
el cómo qué sencillo, qué fulminante el cuándo!

Hat, Overcoat, Gloves

In front of the Comedíe Française is the Regency
Café; in it is a room
set apart, with an easy chair and a table.
When I enter, the unmoving dust has already risen.

Between my rubber lips the cinder
of a cigarette smokes, and in the smoke one sees
two intense smokes, the thorax of the Café
and in the thorax a profound oxide of sadness.

It is important that autumn be grafted to autumns,
important that autumn be composed of sprouts,
the cloud, of half-years; of cheekbones, the wrinkle.

It is important to smell like a madman postulating
how warm the snow is, how fleeting the turtle,
the how hów simple, how fulminant the when!

Altura y Pelos

¿Quién no tiene su vestido azul?
¿Quién no almuerza y no toma el tranvía,
con su cigarrillo contratado y su dolor de bolsillo?
¡Yo que tan sólo he nacido!
¡Yo que tan sólo he nacido!

¿Quién no escribe una carta?
¿Quién no habla de un asunto muy importante,
muriendo de costumbre y llorando de oído?
¡Yo que solamente he nacido!
¡Yo que solamente he nacido!

¿Quién no se llama Carlos o cualquier otra cosa?
¿Quién al gato no dice gato gato?
¡Ay! yo que sólo he nacido solamente!
¡Ay! yo que sólo he nacido solamente!

Height and Hair

Who doesn't have a blue suit?
Who doesn't eat lunch and board the streetcar
with his cigarette bargained for, his pain pocketed?
I who so alone've been born!
I who so alone've been born!

Who doesn't write a letter?
Who doesn't have something very important to say,
dying out of habit and weeping from hearing?
I who've solely been born!
I who've solely been born!

Who isn't called Carlos or anything else?
Who to the cat doesn't say cat cat?
Ay! I who've only been solely born!
Ay! I who've only been solely born!

Me Estoy Riendo

Un guijarro, uno solo, el más bajo de todos,
controla
a todo el médano aciago y faraónico.

El aire adquiere tensión de recuerdo y de anhelo,
y bajo el sol se calla
hasta exigir el cuello a las pirámides.

Sed. Hidratada melancolía de la tribu errabunda
gota
a
gota,
del siglo al minuto.

Son tres. Treses paralelos,
barbados de barba inmemorial,
en marcha 3 3 3

Es el tiempo este anuncio de gran zapatería,
es el tiempo, que marcha descalzo
de la muerte hacia la muerte.

[*Julio 1926*]

I'm Laughing

A pebble, one alone, the deepest,
controls
the whole ominous Pharaonic sand bank.

The air acquires tension of memory and of desire,
and below the sun quiets
until it demands the pyramids' necks.

Thirst. Hydrated melancholy of the wandering tribe,
drop
by
drop,
from century to minute.

They are three. Parallel threes,
beardeds with immemorial beards,
on their way   3   3   3

It's time this sign of a great shoe store,
time that goes on barefoot
from death   toward   death.

La Violencia de las Horas

Todos han muerto.

Murió doña Antonia, la ronca, que hacía pan barato en el burgo.

Murió el cura Santiago, a quien placía le saludasen los jóvenes y las mozas, respondiéndoles a todos, indistintamente: ¡"Buenos días, Jose! ¡Buenos días, María!"

Murió aquella joven rubia, Carlota, dejando un hijito de meses, que luego también murió, a los ocho días de la madre.

Murió mi tía Albina, que solía cantar tiempos y modos de heredad, en tanto cosía en los corredores, para Isidora, la criada de oficio, la honrosísima mujer.

Murió un viejo tuerto, su nombre no recuerdo, pero dormía al sol de la mañana, sentado ante la puerta del hojalatero de la esquina.

Murió Rayo, el perro de mi altura, herido de un balazo de no se sabe quién.

Murió Lucas, mi cuñado en la paz de las cinturas, de quien me acuerdo cuando llueve y no hay nadie en mi experiencia.

Violence of the Hours

All are dead.

Died Doña Antonia, the wheezer, who made cheap bread in the village.

Died the priest Santiago, who liked to be greeted by the young men and country girls, acknowledging everybody indiscriminately: "Buenos días, José! Buenos días, María!"

Died that fair-haired Carlota, leaving a child of three months, who up and died also, eight days after her.

Died my Aunt Albina, who used to sing about the old days in the sierra while she sewed in the hallways for Isadora, the hired maid, that honorable honorable woman.

Died an old one-eye, whose name I don't remember, but who slept in the morning sun, seated in front of the tinsmith's door.

Died Rayo, dog big as me, shot by lord-knows-who.

Died Lucas, my brother-in-law in the peace of the waists, whom I'm reminded of when it rains and there's no one in my experience.

Murió en mi revólver mi madre, en mi puño mi hermana y mi hermano en mi víscera sangrienta, los tres ligados por un género triste de tristeza, en el mes de agosto de años sucesivos.

Murió el músico Méndez, alto y muy borracho, que solfeaba en su clarinete tocatas melancólicas, a cuyo articulado se dormían las gallinas de mi barrio, mucho antes de que el sol se fuese.

Murió mi eternidad y estoy velándola.

Died in my revolver my mother, in my fist my sister and my brother in my bloody viscera, the three of them tied together by a sad gender of sadness, in the month of August of successive years.

Died the musician Méndez, tall and very drunk, who practiced melancholy toccatas on his clarinet, at whose series of proofs the hens in my ward used to doze off, long before the sun went down.

Died my eternity and I am waking it.

La Rueda del Hambriento

Por entre mis propios dientes salgo humeando,
dando voces, pujando,
bajándome los pantalones . . .
Váca mi estómago, váca mi yeyuno,
la miseria me saca por entre mis propios dientes,
cogido con un palito por el puño de la camisa.

Una piedra en que sentarme
¿no habrá ahora para mí?
Aun aquella piedra en que tropieza la mujer que ha dado a luz,
la madre del cordero, la causa, la raíz,
¿ésa no habrá ahora para mí?
¡Siquiera aquella otra,
que ha pasado agachándose por mi alma!
Siquiera
la calcárida o la mala (humilde océano)
o la que ya no sirve ni para ser tirada contra el hombre,
¡ésa dádmela ahora para mí!

Siquiera la que hallaren atravesada y sola en un insulto,
¡ésa dádmela ahora para mí!
Siquiera la torcida y coronada, en que resuena
solamente una vez el andar de las rectas conciencias,
o, al menos, esa otra, que arrojada en digna curva,
va a caer por sí misma,

The Starving Man's Rack

From between my own teeth I come out smoking,
shouting, pushing,
pulling down my pants . . .
My stomach empties, my jejunum empties,
want pulls me out from between my own teeth
caught with a sliver by the cuff of my shirt.

A stone to sit down on,
isn't there even that for me?
Even that stone that trips the woman who's given birth,
mother of the lamb, the cause, the root,
not even that for me now?
At least that other
that passed crouching through my soul!
At least
the calcaretic or the sick (modest ocean)
or that no good now even to throw at man,
that one, give me that one, now, for me!

At least the one they found in the way and only in an insult,

that one, give me that one, now, for me!
At least the twisted and crowned, in which echoes
only once the walk of erect conscience,
or, at least, that other, that flung in upright curve

en profesión de entraña verdadera,
¡ésa dádmela ahora para mí!

Un pedazo de pan, ¿tampoco habrá ahora para mí?
Ya no más he de ser lo que siempre he de ser,
pero dadme
una piedra en que sentarme,
pero dadme,
por favor, un pedazo de pan en que sentarme,
pero dadme
en español
algo, en fin, de beber, de comer, de vivir, de reposarse,
y después me iré . . .
Hallo una extraña forma, está muy rota
y sucia mi camisa
y ya no tengo nada, esto es horrendo.

will drop by itself
professing true center,
that one, give me that one, now, for me!

A piece of bread—that too denied to me?
Now I no longer have to be what I always have to be,
but give me
a stone to sit down on
but give me
por favor, a piece of bread to sit down on
but give me
in Spanish
something, in the end, to drink, to eat, to live, to let me sleep,
then I'll go away . . .
I find a strange form, my shirt's
all ripped and filthy –
and now I have nothing, this is horror.

Los mineros salieron de la mina
remontando sus ruinas venideras,
fajaron su salud con estampidos
y, elaborando su función mental,
cerraron con sus voces
el socavón, en forma de síntoma profundo.

¡Era de ver sus polvos corrosivos!
¡Era de oír sus óxidos de altura!
Cuñas de boca, yunques de boca, aparatos de boca (¡Es formidable!)

El orden de sus túmulos,
sus inducciones plásticas, sus respuestas corales,
agolpáronse al pie de ígneos percances
y airente amarillura conocieron los trístidos y tristes,
imbuidos
del metal que se acaba, del metaloide pálido y pequeño.

Craneados de labor,
y calzados de cuero de vizcacha,
calzados de senderos infinitos,
y los ojos de físico llorar,
creadores de la profundidad,
saben, a cielo intermitente de escalera,
bajar mirando para arriba,
saben subir mirando para abajo.

The miners came out of the mine
going back to their future ruins,
they girded their health with blasts
and elaborating their mental function
closed with their voices
the shaft, shaped a profound symptom.

Just to have seen their corrosive dusts!
Just to have heard their soaring oxides!
Mouthwedges, mouthanvils, mouthapparatus (Tremendous!)
The order of their tumuli,
their plastic inductions, their choral replies
wedged together at the foot of incendiary perquisites
and airish yellowedness they knew, the saddened and the sad, ingrained
with the terminal metal, the pallid ignoble metalloid.

Skulled from labor
and shod with viscacha-hide,
shod with infinite paths
and eyes of physical crying,
creators of the profundity
they know from the ladder's intermittent sky
to climb down looking up,
they know to climb up looking down.

¡Loor al antiguo juego de su naturaleza,
a sus insomnes órganos, a su saliva rústica!
¡Temple, filo y punta, a sus pestañas!
¡Crezcan la yerba, el líquen y la rana en sus adverbios!
¡Felpa de hierro a sus nupciales sábanas!
¡Mujeres hasta abajo, sus mujeres!
¡Mucha felicidad para los suyos!
¡Son algo portentoso, los mineros
remontando sus ruinas venideras,
elaborando su función mental
y abriendo con sus voces
el socavón, en forma de síntoma profundo!
¡Loor a su naturaleza amarillenta,
a su linterna mágica,
a sus cubos y rombos, a sus percances plásticos,
a sus ojazos de seis nervios ópticos
y a sus hijos que juegan en la iglesia
y a sus tácitos padres infantiles!
¡Salud, oh creadores de la profundidad! . . . (Es formidable)

Praise for the ancient game of their nature,
for their sleepless organs, for their rural saliva!
Temper, edge and point, for their eyelashes!
Let grass lichen and frog abound in their adverbs!
Iron plush for their marriage sheets!
Women all the way down, their women!
My best wishes to their people!
They're something prodigious those miners
going back to their future ruins,
elaborating their mental function
and opening with their voices
the shaft, shaped a profound symptom!
Praise for their yellowish nature,
for their magic lantern,
praise for their cubes and rhombs, for their plastic perquisites,
praise for their cyclopt eyes of six optical nerves
and for their children who play in the church
and for their tacit infantile fathers!
Hail, oh creators of the profundity! . . . (Tremendous)

He aquí que hoy saludo, me pongo el cuello y vivo,
superficial de pasos insondable de plantas.
Tal me recibo de hombre, tal más bien me despido
y de cada hora mía retoña una distanciA.

¿Queréis más? encantado.
Políticamente, mi palabra
emite cargos contra mi labio inferior
y económicamente,
cuando doy la espalda a Oriente,
distingo en dignidad de muerte a mis visitas.

Desde ttttales códigos regulares saludo
al soldado desconocido
al verso perseguido por la tinta fatal
y al saurio que Equidista diariamente
de su vida y su muerte,
como quien no hace la cosa.

El tiempo tiene hun miedo ciempiés a los relojes.

(*Los lectores pueden poner el título que quieran a este poema.*)

[*Octubre 1926*]

It's here today I greet, I fix on my collar and live,
step superficial sole fathomless.
So do I graduate as a man, or rather I take leave
and from each of my hours a distance sproutS.

You want more? with pleasure.
Politically, my word
spreads charges against my lower lip
and economically,
when I turn my back to the Orient,
I distinguish my visits in mortal dignity.

According tttto such common code I greet
the unknown soldier
the line pursued by fatal ink
and the saurian that Equidists daily
from its life and its death,
as one who is here and could care less.

Time has úh céntipedal fear of clocks.

(The reader can put whatever title he likes to this poem.)

Salutación Angélica

Eslavo con respecto a la palmera,
alemán de perfil al sol, inglés sin fin,
francés en cita con los caracoles,
italiano ex profeso, escandinavo de aire,
español de pura bestia, tal el cielo
ensartado en la tierra por los vientos,
tal el beso del límite en los hombros.

Mas sólo tú demuestras, descendiendo
o subiendo del pecho, bolquevique,
tus trazos confundibles,
tu gesto marital,
tu cara de padre,
tus piernas de amado,
tu cutis por teléfono,
tu alma perpendicular
a la mía,
tus codos de justo
y un pasaporte en blanco en tu sonrisa.

Obrando por el hombre, en nuestras pausas,
matando, tú, a lo largo de tu muerte
y a lo ancho de un abrazo salubérrimo,
ví que cuando comías, después, tenías gusto,
ví que en tus sustantivos creció yerba.

Angelic Greeting

Slav with respect to the palm tree,
German profile to the sun, English without end,
French while rendezvousing with the snails,
Italian avowedly, Scandinavian to the air,
Spanish out of pure stubbornness – thus the sky
strung on the earth by the winds,
thus the kiss of the limit on the shoulders.

But you alone, Bolshevik, demonstrate
descending or rising from your chest
your confusable characteristics,
your marital gesture,
your fatherly face,
your lover-like legs,
your skin over the telephone,
soul
perpendicular to mine,
elbows of one who is just,
a blank passport in your smile.

Working for man, during our breaks,
killing, you, along your death
and across a "lost brother" embrace,
I saw when you ate, after, you had taste,
I saw in your substantives grass.

Yo quisiera, por eso,
tu calor doctrinal, frío y en barras,
tu añadida manera de mirarnos
y aquesos tuyos pasos metalúrgicos,
aquesos tuyos pasos de otra vida.

Y digo, bolchevique, tomando esta flaqueza
en su feroz liniaje de exhalación terrestre:
hijo natural del bien y del mal
y viviendo talvez por vanidad, para que digan,
me dan tus simultáneas estaturas mucha pena,
puesto que tú no ignoras en quién se me hace tarde diariamente,
en quién estoy callado y medio tuerto.

[*Vers 1931*]

Therefore I'd like
your doctrinal warmth, cold and in bars,
your added way of looking at us
and those metallurgic steps of yours,
those steps of yours of other life.

And I speak, Bolshevik, taking this weakness
in its ferocious lineage of earthly exhalation:
bastard son of good and evil
living perhaps by vanity, in order that théy say,
your simultaneous statures make me very sad,
for you're not unaware of who grows late to me daily,
in who I am silent and half one-eyed.

Por último, sin ese buen aroma sucesivo,
sin él,
sin su cuociente melancólico,
cierra su manto mi ventaja suave,
mis condiciones cierran sus cajitas.

¡Ay, cómo la sensación arruga tanto!
¡ay, cómo una idea fija me ha entrado en una uña!

Albino, áspero, abierto, con temblorosa hectárea,
mi deleite cae viernes,
mas mi triste tristumbre se compone de cólera y tristeza
y, a su borde arenoso e indoloro,
la sensación me arruga, me arrincona.

Ladrones de oro, víctimas de plata:
el oro que robara yo a mis víctimas,
¡rico de mí olvidándolo!
la plata que robara a mis ladrones,
¡pobre de mí olvidándolo!

Execrable sistema, clima en nombre del cielo, del bronquio
y la quebrada,
la cantidad enorme de dinero que cuesta el ser pobre . . .

Ultimately, without that good repetitive aroma,
without it,
without its melancholy quotient,
my slight advantage closes its cloak,
my conditions close their little boxes.

Ay how the feeling really wrinkles!
Ay like a fixed idea forced in under my nail!

Albino, severe, open, acre trembling,
my pleasure falls Friday,
yet my sad doomed sadness consists of anger and sadness
and, at its painless sandy edge,
the feeling wrinkles me, corners me.

Thieves of gold, victims of silver:
the gold I stole from my victim,
        rich me if I forget it,
the silver I stole from my thieves,
        poor me if I forget it!

Execrable system, climate in name of the sky, of the
        bronchus and the gorge,
the enormous quantity of money it costs the poor béing . . .

Epistola a los Transeuntes

Reanudo mi día de conejo,
mi noche de elefante en descanso.

Y, entre mí, digo:
ésta es mi inmensidad en bruto, a cántaros,
éste mi grato peso, que me buscara abajo para pájaro;
éste es mi brazo
que por su cuenta rehusó ser ala,
éstas son mis sagradas escrituras,
éstos mis alarmados compañones.

Lúgubre isla me alumbrará continental,
mientras el capitolio se apoye en mi íntimo derrumbe
y la asamblea en lanzas clausure mi desfile.

Pero cuando yo muera
de vida y no de tiempo,
cuando lleguen a dos mis dos maletas,
éste ha de ser mi estómago en que cupo mi lámpara en
pedazos,
ésta aquella cabeza que expió los tormentos del círculo en mis
pasos,
éstos esos gusanos que el corazón contó por unidades,
éste ha de ser mi cuerpo solidario
por el que vela el alma individual; éste ha de ser
mi ombligo en que maté mis piojos natos,
ésta mi cosa cosa, mi cosa tremebunda.

Epistle to the Pedestrians

I resume my rabbit day,
my night of an elephant in repose.

And to myself I say
This is my immensity in the raw, in bucketfuls,
this my delightful weight that looked under me for a bird;
this is my arm
that on its own refused to be wing;
these are my scriptures,
these my alarmed balls.

Lugubrious isle will illuminate me continental
while City Hall leans on my intimate collapse
and the assembly closes my parade in spears.

But when I die of
life, and not of time,
when my two suitcases come to two,
this will be my stomach in which I fit my shattered lantern
glass,
this that head that expiated the circular torment in my steps,
these those worms my heart counted out one by one,
this will be my solidary body
over which the individual soul keeps watch; this will be
my navel in which I cracked my born lice,
this my thing thing, my dreadful thing.

En tanto, convulsiva, ásperamente
convalece mi freno,
sufriendo como sufro del lenguaje directo del león:
y, puesto que he existido entre dos potestades de ladrillo,
convalezco yo mismo, sonriendo de mis labios.

Meanwhile, convulsively, harshly,
my brake convalesces,
suffering like I suffer the direct language of the lion;
and since I've existed between two brick powers
I myself convalesce smiling at my lips.

Quisiera hoy ser feliz de buena gana,
ser feliz y portarme frondoso de preguntas,
abrir por temperamento de par en par mi cuarto, como loco,
y reclamar, en fin,
en mi confianza física acostado,
sólo por ver si quieren,
sólo por ver si quieren probar de mi espontánea posición,
reclamar, voy diciendo,
por qué me dan así tanto en el alma.

Pues quisiera en sustancia ser dichoso,
obrar sin bastón, laica humildad, ni burro negro.
Así las sensaciones de este mundo,
los cantos subjuntivos,
el lápiz que perdí en mi cavidad
y mis amados órganos de llanto.

Hermano persuasible, camarada,
padre por la grandeza, hijo mortal,
amigo y contendor, inmenso documento de Darwin:
¿A qué hora, pues, vendrán con mi retrato?
¿A los goces? ¿Acaso sobre goce amortajado?
¿Más temprano? ¿Quién sabe, a las porfías?

Today I'd really like to be happy,
to bé happy and burst into question,
to open as I damn please wide open, wildly, my room and
demand, in short,
laid out on my physical trust,
only through seeing if they'd like,
only through seeing if they'd like to try my spontaneous position, and
demand I keep saying
why they've struck me só much in the soul.

For I'd like briefly to live happy,
to work without a cane, without laic humility or black burro.
Thus the sensations of this world,
the subjunctive songs,
the pencil I lost in my cavity
and my beloved organs for crying.

Brother I might win over, comrade,
father through grandeur, mortal son,
friend and opponent, immense document of Darwin:
At what hour then will they come with my portrait?
At fruition? Perhaps after fruition shrouded?
Earlier? Who knows, by the rounds?

A las misericordias, camarada,
hombre mío en rechazo y observación, vecino
en cuyo cuello enorme sube y baja,
al natural, sin hilo, mi esperanza . . .

Out of mercy, comrade,
man like myself in rejection and observation, neighbor
in whose enormous neck rises and lowers
inherently, threadbare, my hope . . .

Considerando en frío, imparcialmente,
que el hombre es triste, tose y, sin embargo,
se complace en su pecho colorado;
que lo único que hace es componerse
de días;
que es lóbrego mamífero y se peina . . .

Considerando
que el hombre procede suavemente del trabajo
y repercute jefe, suena subordinado;
que el diagrama del tiempo
es constante diorama en sus medallas
y, a medio abrir, sus ojos estudiaron,
desde lejanos tiempos,
su fórmula famélica de masa . . .

Comprendiendo sin esfuerzo
que el hombre se queda, a veces pensando,
como queriendo llorar,
y, sujeto a tenderse como objeto,
se hace buen carpintero, suda, mata
y luego canta, almuerza, se abotona . . .

Considerando también
que el hombre es en verdad un animal
y, no obstante, al voltear, me da con su tristeza en la cabeza . . .

Considering coldly, impartially,
that man is sad, coughs and, however
takes pleasure in his reddened chest;
that the only thing he does is to be made
of days;
that he's a gloomy mammal and combs himself . . .

Considering
that man proceeds softly from work
and reverberates boss, sounds employee;
that the diagram of time
is constant diorama on his medals
and, half open, his eyes have studied
since distant times
his famished mass formula . . .

Understanding easily
that man stops, at times, and thinks
like wanting to cry,
and given to stretching out like an object
makes himself a good carpenter, sweats, kills
and then sings, lunches, buttons up . . .

Considering too
that man is in truth an animal
and notwithstanding turning hits me on the head with his sadness . . .

Examinando, en fin,
sus encontradas piezas, su retrete,
su desesperación, al terminar su día atroz, borrándolo . . .

Comprendiendo
que él sabe que le quiero,
que le odio con afecto y me es, en suma, indiferente . . .

Considerando sus documentos generales
y mirando con lentes aquel certificado
que prueba que nació muy pequeñito . . .

le hago una seña,
viene,
y le doy un abrazo, emocionado.
¡Qué más da! Emocionado . . . Emocionado . . .

Examining, finally,
his opposed chunks, his stool,
his desperation at the end of his atrocious day, rubbing it out . . .

Understanding
that he knows I love him,
that I hate him with affection and to me he is in sum indifferent . . .

Considering his general documents
and scrutinizing that certificate
that proves he was born very teeny . . .

I signal him,
he comes,
and I embrace him, moved.
So what! Moved . . . Moved . . .

Gleba

Con afecto mundial de vela que se enciende,
el prepucio directo, hombres a golpes,
funcionan los labriegos a tiro de neblina,
con alabadas barbas,
pie práctico y reginas sinceras de los valles.

¡Hablan como les vienen las palabras,
cambian ideas bebiendo
orden sacerdotal de una botella;
cambian también ideas tras de un árbol, parlando
de escrituras privadas, de la luna menguante
y de los ríos públicos! (¡Inmenso! ¡Inmenso! ¡Inmenso!)

Función de fuerza
sorda y de zarza ardiendo,
paso de palo,
gesto de palo,
acápites de palo,
la palabra colgando de otro palo.

De sus hombros arranca, carne a carne, la herramienta
florecida,
de sus rodillas bajan ellos mismos por etapas hasta el cielo,
y, agitando
y
agitando sus faltas en forma de antiguas calaveras,

Glebe

With universal affection of a candle that bursts into flame,
prepuce right off, men blow by blow,
the peasants function within shot of the fog,
beards extolled,
practical feet, true reigners of the valleys.

They speak when words come,
exchange ideas drinking
sacerdotal order from a bottle;
they exchange ideas too behind a tree, chatting
about private writings, about the moon waning
about the public rivers! (Immense! Immense! Immense!)

Function of blind
strength, man a burning bush,
stick step,
stick gesture,
stick headings,
on another stick the word hung.

From their shoulders flesh by flesh the flowered tool roots
out,
from their knees they go down themselves stage by stage to sky,
and, fluttering
and
fluttering their lacks shaped like antique skulls

levantan sus defectos capitales con cintas,
su mansedumbre y sus
vasos sanguíneos, tristes, de jueces colorados.

Tienen su cabeza, su tronco, sus extremidades,
tienen su pantalón, sus dedos metacarpos y un palito;
para comer vistiéronse de altura
y se lavan la cara acariciándose con sólidas palomas.

Por cierto aquestos hombres
cumplen años en los peligros,
echan toda la frente en sus salutaciones;
carecen de reloj, no se jactan jamás de respirar
y, en fin, suelen decirse: Allá, las putas, Luís Taboada, los ingleses;
¡allá ellos, allá ellos, allá ellos!

they raise their capital failings with black ribbons,
their meekness and their
sad sanguine arteries of reddened judges.

They have their head, their trunk, their extremities,
their trousers, their metacarpal fingers and a little stick;
in order to eat they dressed in height
and they wash their faces caressing themselves with solid doves.

Of course these men
pile up years in risks,
they throw out their entire forehead in a greeting;
they lack watches, they never never brag about breathing;
in short, they're used to telling themselves: To hell with the
whores, with Luís Taboada, with the Englishmen;
to hell with them, to hell with them, to hell with them!

Cesa el anhelo, rabo al aire. De súbito, la vida se amputa, en seco. Mi propia sangre me salpica en líneas femeninas, y hasta la misma urbe sale a ver esto que se pára de improviso.

—¿Qué ocurre aquí, en este hijo del hombre? —clama la urbe, y en una sala del Louvre, un niño llora de terror a la vista del retrato de otro niño.

—¿Qué ocurre aquí, en este hijo de mujer? —clama la urbe, y en una estatua del siglo de los Ludovico, le nace una brizna de yerba en plena palma de la mano.

Cesa el anhelo, a la altura de la mano enarbolada. Y yo me escondo detrás de mí mismo, a aguaitarme si paso por lo bajo o merodeo en alto.

Longing quits, tail to the air. Suddenly life is amputated, that's it. My own blood spatters me in feminine lines and the whole city's out to see this that stops without warning.

–What's going on here in this son of man, the city shouts, and in a room of the Louvre a child weeps in terror at the sight of another child's portrait.

–What's going on here in this son of woman, the city shouts, and in a statue from the Ludwigan century a grass blade is born right in the palm of its hand.

Longing quits at the height of the thrust-up hand. And I hide in back of myself peeking out to see if I pass behind my back or head on on high.

Una mujer de senos apacibles, ante los que la lengua de la vaca resulta una glándula violenta. Un hombre de templanza, mandibular de genio, apto para marchar de a dos con los goznes de los cofres. Un niño está al lado del hombre, llevando por el revés, el derecho animal de la pareja.

¡Oh la palabra del hombre, libre de adjetivos y de adverbios, que la mujer declina en su único caso de mujer, aun entre las mil voces de la Capilla Sixtina! ¡Oh la falda de ella, en el punto maternal donde pone el pequeño las manos y juega a los pliegues, haciendo a veces agrandar las pupilas de la madre, como en las sanciones de los confesionarios!

Yo tengo mucho gusto de ver así al Padre, al Hijo y al Espiritusanto, con todos los emblemas e insignias de sus cargos.

A woman with peaceful breasts, before which the cow's tongue becomes a violent gland. A man of temperance, with a mandibular disposition, ready to march side by side with the hinges of the coffers. A child is at the man's side, wearing wrong side out the animal right of the couple.

O the word of man, free from adjectives and adverbs, that woman declines in her singular case of woman, even among the thousand voices of the Sistine Chapel! O that woman's skirt, right at the maternal point on which the little one puts his hands and plays with the pleats, at times making his mother's eyes dilate as in the sanction of the confessional!

I am very very glad to see the Father, the Son and the Holy Spirit like this, with all the emblems and insignia of their offices.

El Momento mas Grave de la Vida

Un hombre dijo:

—El momento más grave de mi vida estuvo en la batalla del Marne, cuando fuí herido en el pecho.

Otro hombre dijo:

—El momento más grave de mi vida, ocurrió en un maremoto de Yokohama, del cual salvé milagrosamente, refugiado bajo el alero de una tienda de lacas.

Y otro hombre dijo:

—El momento más grave de mi vida acontece cuando duermo de día.

Y otro dijo:

—El momento más grave de mi vida ha estado en mi mayor soledad.

Y otro dijo:

—El momento más grave de mi vida fue mi prisión en una cárcel del Perú.

The Most Perilous Moment in Life

A man said:

—The most perilous moment in my life was in the battle of the Marne when I was struck in the chest.

Another man said:

—The most perilous moment in my life occurred during a Yokohama seaquake, from which I was miraculously saved, sheltered under the eaves of a lacquer shop.

And another man said:

—The most perilous moment in my life happens when I sleep during the day.

And another said:

—The most perilous moment in my life has been in my greatest loneliness.

And another said:

—The most perilous moment in my life was my imprisonment in a Peruvian jail.

Y otro dijo:

–El momento más grave de mi vida es el haber sorprendido de perfil a mi padre.

Y el último hombre dijo:

El momento más grave de mi vida no ha llegado todavía.

And another said:

—The most perilous moment in my life is the having surprised my father in profile.

And the last man said:

—The most perilous moment in my life is yet to come.

—No vive ya nadie en la casa —me dices—; todos se han ido. La sala, el dormitorio, el patio yacen despoblados. Nadie ya queda, pues que todos han partido.

Y yo te digo: Cuando alguien se va alguien queda. El punto por donde pasó un hombre, ya no está solo. Unicamente está solo, de soledad humana, el lugar por donde ningún hombre ha pasado. Las casas nuevas están más muertas que las viejas, por que sus muros son de piedra o de acero, pero no de hombres. Una casa viene al mundo, no cuando la acaban de edificar, sino cuando empiezan a habitarla. Una casa vive únicamente de hombres, como una tumba. De aquí esa irresistible semejanza que hay entre una casa y una tumba. Sólo que la casa se nutre de la vida del hombre, mientras que la tumba se nutre de la muerte del hombre. Por eso la primera está de pie, mientras que la segunda está tendida.

Todas han partido de la casa, en realidad, pero todos se han quedado en verdad. Y no es el recuerdo de ellos lo que queda, sino ellos mismos. Y no es tampoco que ellos queden en la casa, sino que continúan por la casa. Las funciones y los actos, se van de la casa en tren o en avión o a caballo, a pie o arrastrándose. Lo que continúa en la casa es el órgano, el agente en gerundio y en círculo. Los pasos se han ido, los besos, los perdones, los crímenes. Lo que continúa en la casa es el pie, los labios, los ojos, el corazón. Las negaciones y las afirmaciones, el bien y el mal, se han dispersado. Lo que continúa en la casa, es el sujeto del acto.

–No one lives in the house anymore – you tell me –; all have gone. The parlor, the bedroom, the patio lie deserted. No one remains, everyone's gone.

And I say to you: when someone goes someone remains. The point where a man passed is no longer alone. Only that place is alone, from human solitude, where no man has passed. New houses are deader than old ones, for their walls are of stone or steel but not of men. A house comes into the world not when it is built but when people begin to inhabit it. A house lives only off men, like a tomb. Behold that irresistible resemblance between house and tomb. Only that the house is nourished by the life of man, while the tomb is nourished by his death. Therefore the first is standing; the second laid out.

All have actually parted from the house, but all truly have remained. And it's not the memory of them that remains, but they themselves. Nor is it that they remain in the house but that they continue because of the house. The functions and the acts go from the house by train or by plane or on horseback, walking or crawling. What continues in the house is the organ, the gerundial or circular agent. The steps, the kisses, the pardons, the crimes have gone. What continues in the house is the foot, the lips, the eyes, the heart. Negations and affirmations, good and evil, have scattered. What continues in the house is the subject of the act.

Entre el dolor y el placer median tres criaturas,
de las cuales la una mira a un muro,
la segunda usa de ánimo triste
y la tercera avanza de puntillas;
pero, entre tú y yo,
sólo existen segundas criaturas.

Apoyándose en mi frente, el día
conviene en que, de veras,
hay mucho de exacto en el espacio;
pero, si la dicha, que, al fin, tiene un tamaño,
principia, ¡ay! por mi boca,
¿quién me preguntará por mi palabra?

Al sentido instantáneo de la eternidad
corresponde
este encuentro investido de hilo negro,
pero a tu despedida temporal,
tan sólo corresponde lo inmutable,
tu criatura, el alma, mi palabra.

Between pain and pleasure three children mediate,
of which one looks at a wall,
the second plucks up sad courage
and the third advances on tiptoes;
but, between you and me,
only second children exist.

Resting on my forehead the day
agrees that truthfully
there is much exact in space;
but if the good fortune that in the end has a size
begins, ay! through my mouth,
who will ask me about my word?

To the instantaneous sensing of eternity
corresponds
this meeting invested with black thread,
but to your temporal farewell
only corresponds what is immutable,
your child, the soul, my word.

¡Y si después de tantas palabras,
no sobrevive la palabra!
¡Si después de las alas de los pájaros,
no sobrevive el pájaro parado!
¡Más valdría, en verdad,
que se lo coman todo y acabemos!

¡Haber nacido para vivir de nuestra muerte!
¡Levantarse del cielo hacia la tierra
por sus propios desastres
y espiar el momento de apagar con su sombra su tiniebla!
¡Más valdría, francamente,
que se lo coman todo y qué más da! . . .

¡Y si después de tanta historia, sucumbimos,
no ya de eternidad,
sino de esas cosas sencillas, como estar
en la casa o ponerse a cavilar!
¡Y si luego encontramos,
de buenas a primeras, que vivimos,
a juzgar por la altura de los astros,
por el peine y las manchas del pañuelo!
¡Más valdría, en verdad,
que se lo coman todo, desde luego!

And if after so many words
the word doesn't survive!
If after the bird's wings
the bird standing doesn't survive!
Much better in fact
that they eat it all up, fuck it!

To have been born in order to live off our death!
To get up from sky toward earth
through one's own disasters
and glimpse the moment for putting out one's shadow with one's darkness!
Much better frankly
that they eat it all up, like so what! . . .

And if after so much history we succumb
no longer from eternity
but from those simple things, like being
home or starting to think!
And then if we find
all at once that we live,
to judge by the height of the stars,
by the comb and handkerchief stains!
Much better in fact
that they eat it all up, of course!

Se dirá que tenemos
en uno de los ojos mucha pena
y también en el otro, mucha pena
y en los dos, cuando miran, mucha pena . . .
¡Entonces! . . . ¡Claro! . . . Entonces . . . ¡ni palabra!

It will be said that in one
of our eyes we have much sorrow
and likewise in the other, much sorrow
and in the two, when they look, much sorrow . . .
Then! . . . Of course! . . . Then . . . why bother!

En el momento en que el tenista lanza magistralmente
su bala, le posee una inocencia totalmente animal;
en el momento
en que el filósofo sorprende una nueva verdad,
es una bestia completa.
Anatole France afirmaba
que el sentimiento religioso
es la funcíon de un órgano especial del cuerpo humano,
hasta ahora ignorado y se podría
decir también, entonces,
que, en el momento exacto en que un tal órgano
funciona plenamente
tan puro de malicia está el creyente,
que se diría casi un vegetal.
¡Oh alma! ¡Oh pensamiento! ¡Oh Marx! ¡Oh Feuerbach!

The moment the tennis player magisterially serves
his bullet, a totally animal innocence comes over him;
the moment the philosopher surprises a new truth
he's a complete beast.
Anatole France affirmed
that the religious sentiment
is the function of a special organ in the human body
until now ignored, and one could
say too, then,
that the exact moment such an organ
fully functions
the believer is so full of malice
one could almost call him a vegetable.
O my soul! O my thought! O Marx! O Feuerbach!

Parado en una piedra,
desocupado,
astroso, espeluznante,
a la orilla del Sena, va y viene.
Del río brota entonces la conciencia,
con pecíolo y rasguños de árbol ávido;
del río sube y baja la ciudad, hecha de lobos abrazados.

El parado la ve yendo y viniendo,
monumental, llevando sus ayunos en la cabeza cóncava,
en el pecho sus piojos purísimos
y abajo
su pequeño sonido, el de su pelvis,
callado entre dos grandes decisiones,
y abajo,
más abajo,
un papelito, un clavo, una cerilla . . .

¡Este es, trabajadores, aquel
que en la labor sudaba para afuera,
que suda hoy para adentro su secreción de sangre rehusada!
Fundidor del cañón, que sabe cuántas zarpas son acero,
tejedor que conoce los hilos positivos de sus venas,
albañil de pirámides,
constructor de descensos por columnas
serenas, por fracasos triunfales,

Checked on a stone,
out of work,
scroungy, hair-raising,
at the bank of the Seine, it comes and goes.
Conscience, then, sprouts from the river,
with petiole and slashes of the thirsty tree;
from the river rises and lowers the city, made of embraced wolves.

The checked sees it coming and going,
monumental, carrying its fastings on his concave head,
in his chest its purest lice
and below
its small sound, that of his pelvis,
silent between two big decisions,
and below,
further below,
a paperscrap, a nail, a match . . .

This is, workers, that man
who in labor sweated toward the outside,
who today sweats toward the inside his secretion of refused blood!

Cannon founder who knows how many claws are steel,
weaver knowing the positive threads of his veins,
pyramid bricklayer,

parado individual entre treinta millones de parados,
andante en multitud,
¡qué salto el retratado en su talón
y qué humo el de su boca ayuna, y cómo
su talle incide, canto a canto, en su herramienta atroz, parada,
y qué idea de dolorosa válvula en su pómulo!

También parado el hierro frente al horno,
paradas las semillas con sus sumisas síntesis al aire,
parados los petróleos conexos,
parada en sus auténticos apóstrofes la luz,
parados de crecer los laureles,
paradas en un pie las aguas móviles
y hasta la tierra misma, parada de estupor ante este paro,
¡qué salto el retratado en sus tendones!
¡qué transmisión entablan sus cien pasos!
¡cómo chilla el motor en su tobillo!
¡cómo gruñe el reloj, paseándose impaciente a sus espaldas!
¡cómo oye deglutir a los patrones
el trago que le falta, camaradas,
y el pan que se equivoca de saliva,
y, oyéndolo, sintiéndolo, en plural, humanamente,
¡cómo clava el relámpago
su fuerza sin cabeza en su cabeza!
y lo que hacen, abajo, entonces, ¡ay!
¡más abajo, camaradas,
el papelucho, el clavo, la cerilla,
el pequeño sonido, el piojo padre!

builder of descents through serene
columns, through triumphant disasters,
checked individual among thirty million checked,
wandering in multitude,
what leap portrayed in his heel,
what smoke from his fasting mouth, and how
his physical shape coincides, edge to edge, with his atrocious tool, checked,
in his cheekbone what an idea of painful valve!

Likewise checked–iron before its furnace,
seeds checked their humble synthesis bared,
checked the petroleums connected,
checked in its authentic apostrophes the light,
the laurel checked growing,
checked in a foot the mobile waters
and even the earth itself, checked from stupor before this check,
what leap portrayed in his tendons!
what transmission his hundred steps jam!
how the motor screams in his ankle!
how the clock grinds cycling impatiently in his back!
how he hears the owners gulp
down the shot he lacks, comrades,
and the bread mistaking the saliva,
hearing it, feeling it, in plural, humanly,
how lightning nails
its headless force into his head!
and what they do below then, aie!
further below, comrades,
the dirtyscrap, the nail, the match,
the small sound, the father louse!

Hasta el día en que vuelva, de esta piedra
nacerá mi talón definitivo,
con su juego de crímenes, su yedra,
su obstinación dramática, su olivo.

Hasta el día en que vuelva, prosiguiendo,
con franca rectitud de cojo amargo,
de pozo en pozo, mi periplo, entiendo
que el hombre ha de ser bueno, sin embargo.

Hasta el día en que vuelva y hasta que ande
el animal que soy, entre sus jueces,
nuestro bravo meñique será grande,
digno, infinito dedo entre los dedos.

Until the day it returns, from this stone
my definitive heel will burgeon,
with its game of crimes, its ivy,
its dramatic stubbornness, its olive.

Until the day it returns, continuing
with the open uprightness of a bitter cripple
from well to well, my circumnavigation, I understand man has to be good, howéver.

Until the day it returns and until it walks
animal that I am between its judges,
our brave little finger will be big,
dignified, infinite finger between the fingers.

Pero antes de que se acabe
toda esta dicha, piérdela atajándola,
tómale la medida, por si rebasa tu ademán; rebásala,
ve si cabe tendida en tu extensión.

Bien la sé por su llave,
aunque no sepa, a veces, si esta dicha
anda sola, apoyada en tu infortunio
o tañida, por sólo darte gusto, en tus falanjas.
Bien la sé única, sola
de una sabiduría solitaria.

En tu oreja el cartílago está hermoso
y te escribo por eso, te medito:
no olvides en tu sueño de pensar que eres feliz,
que la dicha es un hecho profundo, cuando acaba,
pero al llegar asume
un caótico aroma de asta muerta.

Silbando a tu muerte,
sombrero a la pedrada,
blanco, ladeas a ganar tu batalla de escaleras,
soldado del tallo, filósofo del grano, mecánico del sueño.
(¿Me percibes, animal?
¿me dejo comparar como tamaño?

But before all this good luck
ends, lose it cutting it short,
measure it, in case it overflows your gesture; overflow it,
see if it fits stretched out in your own expanse.

I know it well by its key,
although I don't know, at times, if this good luck
walks alone, leaned on your misfortune
or played, just to tease you, in your phalanges.
I know it well uniquely, alone
from a lonely wisdom.

In your ear the cartilage looks beautiful
and so I write you, I meditate you;
don't forget in your dream to think you are happy,
that good luck is a profound fact, when it ends,
but when it comes it assumes
a chaotic odor of a dead lance.

Whistling at your death,
hat cocked,
a fool, you sway to win your battle of stairs,
soldier of the stalk, philosopher of the grain, mechanic of the dream.

(Do you see me, animal?
do I allow myself to be compared like size?

No respondes y callado me miras
a través de la edad de tu palabra.)

Ladeando así tu dicha, volverá
a clamarla tu lengua, a despedirla,
dicha tan desgraciada de durar.
Antes, se acabará violentamente,
dentada, pedernalina estampa,
y entonces oirás cómo medito
y entonces tocarás cómo tu sombra es ésta mía desvestida
y entonces olerás cómo he sufrido.

You don't answer and silent you look at me
across the age of your word.)

Skirting your good luck this way, again
your tongue will beg for it, to say goodbye to it,
good luck too unlucky to last.
Instead, it'll end violently,
dentated stamped in flint,
and then you'll hear how I meditate
and then you'll touch how your shadow is mine undressed
and then you'll smell how I suffered.

París, Octubre 1936

De todo esto yo soy el único que parte.
De este banco me voy, de mis calzones,
de mi gran situación, de mis acciones,
de mi número hendido parte a parte,
de todo esto yo soy el único que parte.

De los Campos Elíseos o al dar vuelta
la extraña callejuela de la Luna,
mi defunción se va, parte mi cuna,
y, rodeada de gente, sola, suelta,
mi semejanza humana dase vuelta
y despacha sus sombras una a una.

Y me alejo de todo, porque todo
se queda para hacer la coartada:
mi zapato, su ojal, también su lodo
y hasta el doblez del codo
de mi propia camisa abotonada.

Paris, October 1936

From all this I'm the only one who parts.
From this bench I'm off, from my breeches,
from my great situation, from my acts,
from my number split part to part,
from all this I'm the only one who parts.

From the Champs Élysées or as strange
little Moon Street turns around,
my defunction's off, my cradle parts,
and surrounded by people, alone, loose,
my human resemblance turns around
sending out its shadows one by one.

And I remove from everything, for every
thing remains to make my alibi:
my shoe, its buttonhole, likewise its mud—
even the double in the elbow
of my own shirt buttoned up.

Existe un mutilado, no de un combate sino de un abrazo, no de la guerra sino de la paz. Perdió el rostro en el amor y no en el odio. Lo perdió en el curso normal de la vida y no en un accidente. Lo perdió en el orden de la naturaleza y no en el desorden de los hombres. El coronel Piccot, Presidente de "Les gueules cassées," lleva la boca comida por la pólvora de 1914. Este mutilado que conozco, lleva el rostro comido, por el aire inmortal e inmemorial.

Rostro muerto sobre el tronco vivo. Rostro yerto y pegado con clavos a la cabeza viva. Este rostro resulta ser el dorso del cráneo, el cráneo del cráneo. Ví una vez un árbol darme la espalda y ví otra vez un camino que me daba la espalda. Un árbol de espaldas sólo crece en los lugares donde nunca nació ni murió nadie. Un camino de espaldas sólo avanza por los lugares donde ha habido todas las muertes y ningún nacimiento. El mutilado de la paz y del amor, del abrazo y del orden y que lleva el rostro muerto sobre el tronco vivo, nació a la sombra de un árbol de espaldas y su existencia trascurre a lo largo de un camino de espaldas.

Como el rostro está yerto y difunto, toda la vida psíquica, toda la expresión animal de este hombre, se refugia, para traducirse al exterior, en el peludo cráneo, en el tórax y en las extremidades. Los impulsos de su ser profundo, al salir, retroceden del rostro y la respiración, el olfato, la vista, el

Exists a man mutilated not from combat but from an embrace, not from war but from peace. He lost his face in love and not in hate. Lost it in the normal course of events and not in an accident. Lost it in the order of nature and not in the disorder of men. Colonel Piccot, President of "Les gueules cassées," wears his mouth eaten away by the gunpowder of 1914. This cripple I know wears his face eaten away by the immortal and immemorial air.

Face dead on the living trunk. Face stiff and hammered with nails to the living trunk. This face turns out to be the dorsum of the skull, skull of the skull. I once saw a tree turn its back on me and another time I saw a road turn its back on me. A back-turned road only grows in places where nothing was born or no one died. A back-turned road only advances through places where there've been all deaths and no birth. The man mutilated from peace and from love, from embrace and from order and who wears his dead face on his living trunk was born in the shadow of a back-turned tree and his existence elapses along a back-turned road.

As his face is stiff and defunct, all psychic life, all animal expression of this man, in order to move itself out, takes refuge in the hairy skull, in the thorax and in the extremities. The impulses of his profound béing, on going out, back away from his face and his breathing, his sense of smell, his sight, his

oído, la palabra, el resplandor humano de su ser, funcionan y se expresan por el pecho, por los hombros, por el cabello, por las costillas, por los brazos y las piernas y los pies.

Mutilado del rostro, tapado del rostro, cerrado del rostro, este hombre, no obstante, está entero y nada le hace falta. No tiene ojos y ve y llora. No tiene narices y huele y respira. No tiene oídos y escucha. No tiene boca y habla y sonríe. No tiene frente y piensa y se sume en sí mismo. No tiene mentón y quiere y subsiste. Jesús conocía al mutilado de la función, que tenía ojos y no veía y tenía orejas y no oía. Yo conozco al mutilado del órgano, que ve sin ojos y oye sin orejas.

hearing, his speech, the human radiance of his béing function and are expressed through his chest, through his shoulders, through his hair, through his ribs, through his arms and his legs and his feet.

Face cut up, face clogged, face bolted, this man nevertheless is whole, he wants nothing. He has no eyes and he sees and cries. He has no nostrils and he smells and breathes. He has no ears and he hears. No mouth and he talks and smiles. No forehead and he thinks and withdraws into himself. No chin and he desires and subsists. Jesus knew the man whose functions were mutilated, who had eyes and couldn't see and ears and couldn't hear. I know the man whose organs are mutilated, who sees without eyes and hears without ears.

Piensan los Viejos Asnos

Ahora vestiríame
de músico por verle,
chocaría con su alma, sobándole del destino con mi mano,
le dejaría tranquilo, ya que es un alma a pausas,
en fin, le dejaría
posiblemente muerto sobre su cuerpo muerto.

Podría hoy dilatarse en este frío,
podría toser; le ví bostezar, duplicándose en mi oído
su aciago movimiento muscular.
Tal me refiero a un hombre, a su placa positiva
y, ¿por qué no? a su boldo ejecutante,
aquel horrible filamente lujoso;
a su bastón con puño de plata con perrito,
y a los niños
que él dijo eran sus fúnebres cuñados.

Por eso vestiríame hoy de músico,
chocaría con su alma que quedóse mirando a mi materia . . .

¡Mas ya nunca veréle afeitándose al pie de su mañana;
ya nunca, ya jamás, ya para qué!
¡Hay que ver! ¡Qué cosa cosa!
¡qué jamás de jamases su jamás!

Old Asses Thinking

Now I'd dress
up like a musician to see him,
I'd clash with his soul, kneading the destiny with my hand,
I'd leave him alone, since at breaks he is a soul,
in short I'd leave him
over his dead body possibly dead.

He could today expand in this cold,
could cough; I saw him yawn, intensifying in my ear
his ominous muscular movement.
So do I refer to a man, to his positive plate
and, why not? to his *boldo* performing,
that horrible luxurious filament;
to his cane with its little dog silver head
and to the children
he called his funereal brothers-in-law.

So I'd dress up today like a musician,
I'd clash with his soul that stayed watching my matter . . .

But now never will I see him shaving at the foot of his morning;
never, never-again, but why?
Just to see it! What a thing thing!
what an -again of the -agains his -again!

Fué domingo en las claras orejas de mi burro,
de mi burro peruano en el Perú (Perdonen la tristeza)
Mas hoy ya son las once en mi experiencia personal,
experiencia de un solo ojo, clavado en pleno pecho,
de una sola burrada, clavada en pleno pecho,
de una sola hecatombe, clavada en pleno pecho.

Tal de mi tierra veo los cerros retratados,
ricos en burros, hijos de burros, padres hoy de vista,
que tornan ya pintados de creencias,
cerros horizontales de mis penas.

En su estatua, de espalda,
Voltaire cruza su capa y mira el zócalo,
pero el sol me penetra y espanta de mis dientes incisivos
un número crecido de cuerpos inorgánicos.

Y entonces sueño en una piedra
verduzca, diecisiete,
peñasco numeral que he olvidado,
sonido de años en el rumor de aguja de mi brazo,
lluvia y sol en Europa, y ¡cómo toso! ¡cómo vivo!
¡cómo me duele el pelo al columbrar los siglos semanales!
y cómo, por recodo, mi ciclo microbiano,
quiero decir mi trémulo, patriótico peinado.

It was Sunday in the fair ears of my burro,
my Peruvian burro in Peru (Pardon my sadness)
But already it's eleven o'clock in my personal experience,
experience of a single eye nailed right in the chest,
of a single asininity nailed right in the chest,
of a single hecatomb nailed right in the chest.

So from my country I see the portrayed hills
rich in burros, sons of burros, parents today by sight
altering now painted with beliefs,
hills horizontal to my sorrows.

In his statue, back turned,
Voltaire closes his cape and looks at the socle,
but the sun penetrates me and frightens a grown
number of inorganic bodies from my incisors.

Then I dream on a greenish
seventeen stone,
numeral boulder I've forgotten,
sound of years in the murmur of needle of my arm,
rain and sun in Europe, and how I cough! how I live!
how my hair aches me descrying the weekly centuries!
and how, by its swerve, my microbial cycle,
I mean my tremulous patriotic hairdo.

De disturbio en disturbio
subes a acompañarme a estar solo;
y lo comprendo andando de puntillas,
con un pan en la mano, un camino en el pie
y haciendo, negro hasta sacar espuma,
mi perfil su papel espeluznante.

Ya habías disparado para atrás tu violencia
neumática, otra época, mas luego
me sostienes ahora en brazo de honra fúnebre
y sostienes el rumbo de las cosas en brazo de honra fúnebre,
la muerte de las cosas resumida en brazo de honra fúnebre.

Pero, realmente y puesto
que tratamos de la vida,
cuando el hecho de entonces eche crin en tu mano,
al seguir tu rumor como regando,
cuando sufras en suma de kanguro,
olvídame, sosténme todavía, compañero de cantidad pequeña,
azotado de fechas con espinas,
olvídame y sosténme por el pecho,
jumento que te paras en dos para abrazarme;
duda de tu excremeto unos segundos,
observa cómo el aire empieza a ser el cielo levantándose,
hombrecillo,
hombrezuelo,
hombre con taco, quiéreme, acompáñame . . .

From disturbance to disturbance
you rise to accompany me to be alone;
I understand, walking on tiptoes
with bread in hand, road in foot,
letting, so black it foams,
my profile be your hair-raising role.

Already you've fired behind you your pneumatic
violence, another time, but now
you support me now in arm of last rites
and support the course of things in arm of last rites,
the death of things summed up in arm of last rites.

But actually, and since
we talk about life,
when the fact of then pours mane into your hand
following your own little noise like sprinkling,
when you suffer in sum from kangaroo,
forget me, support me still, companion of next to nothing,
flogged by dates with thorns
forget me and support me by the chest,
noble ass that stands on two to embrace me;
doubt your excrement a bit,
observe how the air begins to be sky lifting,
dear little man,
worthless man,
man with a heel, love me, keep me company . . .

Ten presente que un día
ha de cantar un mirlo de sotana
sobre mi tonelada ya desnuda.
(Cantó un mirlo llevando las cintas de mi gramo entre su pico)
Ha de cantar calzado de este sollozo innato,
hombre con taco,
y, simultánea, doloridamente,
ha de cantar calzado de mi paso,
y no oírlo, hombrezuelo, será malo,
será denuesto y hoja,
pesadumbre, trenza, humo quieto.

Perro parado al borde de una piedra
es el vuelo en su curva;
también tenlo presente, hombrón hasta arriba.
Te lo recordarán el peso bajo, de ribera adversa,
el peso temporal, de gran silencio,
más eso de los meses y aquello que regresa de los años.

Keep in mind that one day
a blackbird in cassock will sing
over my tun now naked.
(A blackbird did sing carrying the ribbons of my gram in its
beak)

It will sing shod from this innate sob,
man with a heel,
and, simultaneously, grievously,
it will sing shod from my step;
and not to hear it, worthless man, will be bad,
will be an insult and leaf,
sorrow, braid, quiet smoke.

Dog stopped at the edge of a stone
is the flight in its curve;
keep that in mind too, powerful man until above.
The low weight of an adverse shore will remind you,
the temporal weight, that of great silence,
plus that of the months and that which returns from the years.

Primavera Tuberosa

Esta vez, arrastrando briosa sus pobrezas
al sesgo de mi pompa delantera,
coteja su coturno con mi traspié sin taco,
la primavera exacta de picotón de buitre.

La perdí en cuanto tela de mis despilfarros,
juguéla en cuanto pomo de mi aplauso;
el termómetro puesto, puesto el fin, puesto el gusano,
contusa mi doblez del otro día,
aguardéla al arrullo de un grillo fugitivo
y despedíla uñoso, somático, sufrido.

Veces latentes de astro,
ocasiones de ser gallina negra,
entabló la bandida primavera
con mi chusma de aprietos,
con mis apocamientos en camisa,
mi derecho soviético y mi gorra.

Veces las del bocado lauríneo,
con símbolos, tabaco, mundo y carne,
deglución translaticia bajo palio,
al són de los testículos cantores;
talentoso torrente el de mi suava suavidad,
rebatible a pedradas, ganable con tán sólo suspirar . . .

Tuberous Spring

This time, punctual with her vulture bite,
vigorously dragging her sterility obliquely
across my foremost pomp, spring
with cothurnus confronts my heelless stumble.

I lost her as fabric of my wastefulness,
I gambled her away as flask of my applause;
the thermometer placed, the end placed, the worm placed,
my duplicity of the other day bruised,
I awaited her to the coo of a fugitive cricket
and saw her off naily, somatic, long-suffering.

Times latent with stars,
occasions of being a black hen,
the bandit spring began
with my mob of dilemmas,
with my diffidences in shirt sleeves,
my soviet right and my cap.

Those times of the laurineous mouthful
with symbols, tobacco, world and flesh,
translatory deglutition under pallium
to the sound of the singing testicles;
that talented torrent of my gentle gentleness,
refutable by stonings, gainable with júst a sigh . . .

Flora de estilo, plena,
citada en fangos de honor por rosas auditivas . . .
Respingo, coz, patada sencilla,
triquiñuela adorada . . . Cantan . . . Sudan . . .

Flora of style, complete,
cited in swamps of honor by auditory roses . . .
Shudder, kick, simple boot,
adored little trick . . .   They sing . . .   They sweat . . .

Y no me digan nada,
que uno puede matar perfectamente,
ya que, sudando tinta,
uno hace cuanto puede, no me digan . . .

Volveremos, señores, a vernos con manzanas;
tarde la criatura pasará,
la expresión de Aristóteles armada
de grandes corazones de madera,
la de Heráclito injerta en la de Marx,
la del suave sonando rudamente . . .
Es lo que bien narraba mi garganta:
uno puede matar perfectamente.

Señores,
caballeros, volveremos a vernos sin paquetes;
hasta entonces exijo, exigiré de mi flaqueza
el acento del día, que
según veo, estuvo ya esperándome en mi lecho.
Y exijo del sombrero la infausta analogía del recuerdo,
ya que, a veces, asumo con éxito mi inmensidad llorada,
ya que, a veces, me ahogo en la voz de mi vecino
y padezco
contando en maíces los años,

And don't tell me anything,
that one can kill perfectly,
now that sweating blood
one does what one can, don't tell me . . .

We shall return, gentlemen, to see each other with apples;
late the child will pass,
the expression of Aristotle armed with great
wood hearts, that of Heraclitus
grafted on that of Marx,
that of the gentle sounding crudely . . .
It is what my throat always narrated:
one can kill perfectly.

Gentlemen,
my lords, we shall return to see each other without bundles;
until then I demand, I shall demand of my frailty
the accent of the day, that
as I see, was waiting for me in my bed.
And I demand of the hat memory's fatal analogy
now that, at times, I assume successfully my wept immensity,
now that, at times, I strangle in my neighbor's voice
and hold out
counting kernel by kernel the years,

cepillando mi ropa al son de un muerto
o sentado borracho en mi ataúd . . .

[*Hacia 1937*]

brushing my clothes to the sound of a corpse
or sitting up drunk in my coffin . . .

¡Cuatro conciencias
simultáneas enrédanse en la mía!
¡Si viérais cómo ese movimiento
apenas cabe ahora en mi conciencia!
¡Es aplastante! Dentro de una bóveda
pueden muy bien
adosarse, ya internas o ya externas
segundas bóvedas, mas nunca cuartas;
mejor dicho, sí,
mas siempre y, a lo sumo, cual segundas.
No puedo concebirlo; es aplastante.
Vosotros mismos a quienes inicio en la noción
de estas quatro conciencias simultáneas,
enredadas en una sola, apenas os tenéis
de pie ante mi cuadrúpedo intensivo.
¡Y yo, que le entrevisto (Estoy seguro)!

Four simultaneous
consciousnesses snarl in mine!
If all of you could see how this movement
hardly fits now in my consciousness!
It's crushing! Deep in a vault
they can very well be
set back to back, now internal now external
second vaults, but never fourths;
better said, yes,
but álways and, at most, those seconds.
I can't conceive it; it's crushing.
You yourselves who I initiate in the notion
of these four simultaneous consciousnesses
snarled in only one, barely do you keep
up before my intense quadruped.
And I, who glimpsed him (I'm sure)!

Nomina de Huesos

Se pedía a grandes voces:

—Que muestre las dos manos a la vez.

Y esto no fué posible.

—Que, mientras llora, le tomen la medida de sus pasos.

Y esto no fué posible.

—Que piense un pensamiento idéntico, en el tiempo en que un cero permanece inútil.

Y esto no fué posible.

—Que haga una locura.

Y esto no fué posible.

—Que entre él y otro hombre semejante a él, se interponga una muchedumbre de hombres como él.

Y esto no fué posible.

—Que le comparen consigo mismo.

Y esto no fué posible.

—Que le llamen, en fin, por su nombre.

Y esto no fué posible.

Bone Catalogue

The multitude shouted:
—Let him show both hands at once.
And this was not possible.
—Let them measure his steps while he weeps.
And this was not possible.
—Let him think an identical thought in the time it takes a zero to lie useless.
And this was not possible.
—Let him do something crazy.
And this was not possible.
—Let between him and another man similar to him a crowd of men like him intercede.
And this was not possible.
—Let them compare him with himself.
And this was not possible.
—Let them call him at last by his name.
And this was not possible.

Voy a Hablar de la Esperanza

Yo no sufro este dolor como César Vallejo. Yo no me duelo ahora como artista, como hombre ni como simple ser vivo siquiera. Yo no sufro este dolor como católico, como mahometano ni como ateo. Hoy sufro solamente. Si no me llamase César Vallejo, también sufriría este mismo dolor. Si no fuese artista, también lo sufriría. Si no fuese hombre ni ser vivo siquiera, también lo sufriría. Si no fuese católico, ateo ni mahometano, también lo sufriría. Hoy sufro desde más abajo. Hoy sufro solamente.

Me duelo ahora sin explicaciones. Mi dolor es tan hondo, que no tuvo ya causa ni carece de causa. ¿Qué sería su causa? ¿Dónde está aquello tan importante, que dejase de ser su causa? Nada es su causa; nada ha podido dejar de ser su causa. ¿A qué ha nacido este dolor, por sí mismo? Mi dolor es del viento del norte y del viento del sur, como esos huevos neutros que algunas aves raras ponen del viento. Si hubiera muerto mi novia, mi dolor sería igual. Si me hubieran cortado el cuello de raíz, mi dolor sería igual. Si la vida fuese, en fin, de otro modo, mi dolor sería igual. Hoy sufro desde más arriba. Hoy sufro solamente.

Miro el dolor del hambriento y veo que su hambre anda tan lejos de mi sufrimiento, que de quedarme ayuno hasta morir, saldría siempre de mi tumba una brizna de yerba al menos. ¡Lo mismo el enamorado! ¡Qué sangre la suya más engendrada, para la mía sin fuente ni consumo!

I Am Going to Speak of Hope

I don't suffer this pain as César Vallejo. I don't ache now as an artist, as a man or even as a simple living being. I don't suffer this pain as a Catholic, as a Mohammedan or as an atheist. Today I just suffer. If I were not called César Vallejo, I'd still suffer this same pain. If I were not an artist, I'd still suffer it. If I were not a man or even a living being, I'd still suffer it. Today I suffer from the depths. Today I simply suffer.

I ache now without any excuses. My pain is so deep it had no cause nor does it lack cause. What could be its cause? Where is that thing so important that its cause could cease to be its cause? Nothing is its cause; nothing has been able to stop being its cause. Why has this pain been born—for itself? My pain comes from the north wind, from the south wind, like those neuter eggs some rare birds lay in the wind. If my bride were dead my pain would be the same. If they cut my throat out by its roots my pain would be the same. If life were finally of a different order, my pain would be the same. Today I suffer from the heights. Today I simply suffer.

I look at the starving man's misery and see his hunger is so distant from my suffering, that if I were to fast unto death, a blade of grass would always sprout from my tomb at least. The same thing happens to the lover! How engendered his blood is compared to mine, my blood without spring or drinker!

Yo creía hasta ahora que todas las cosas del universo eran, inevitablemente, padres o hijos. Pero he aquí que mi dolor de hoy no es padre ni es hijo. Le falta espalda para anochecer, tanto como le sobra pecho para amanecer y si lo pusiesen en la estancia oscura, no daría luz y si lo pusiesen en una estancia luminosa, no echaría sombra. Hoy sufro suceda lo que suceda. Hoy sufro solamente.

I believed until now that all the things of the universe were inevitably fathers or sons. But behold, my pain today is neither father nor son. It lacks a back to darken, just as it has too much chest to dawn, and if they put it in the dark dwelling place it could not give light and if they put it in a lighted dwelling place it would cast no shadow. Today I suffer no matter what happens. Today I simply suffer.

Las ventanas se han estremecido, elaborando una metafísica del universo. Vidrios han caído. Un enfermo lanza su queja: la mitad por su boca lenguada y sobrante, y toda entera, por el ano de su espalda.

Es el huracán. Un castaño del jardín de las Tullerías habráse abatido, al soplo del viento, que mide ochenta metros por segundo. Capiteles de los barrios antiguos, habrán caído, hendiendo, matando.

¿De qué punto interrogo, oyendo a ambas riberas de los océanos, de qué punto viene este huracán, tan digno de crédito, tan honrado de deuda, derecho a las ventanas del hospital? ¡Ay las dirécciones inmutables, que oscilan entre el huracán y esta pena directa de toser o defecar! ¡Ay las direcciones inmutables, que así prenden muerte en las entrañas del hospital y despiertan células clandestinas, a deshora, en los cadáveres!

¿Qué pensaría de sí el enfermo de enfrente, ése que está durmiendo, si hubiera percibido el huracán? El pobre duerme, boca arriba, a la cabeza de su morfina, a los pies de toda su cordura. Un adarme más o menos en la dosis y le llevarán a enterrar, el vientre roto, la boca arriba, sordo al huracán, sordo a su vientre roto, ante el cual suelen los médicos dialogar y cavilar largamente, para, al fin, pronunciar sus llanas palabras de hombres.

The windows have been shaken, elaborating a metaphysic of the universe. Glass has fallen. A sick man launches his cry: half through his tongued and surplus mouth, and completely intact through the anus of his back.

It's the hurricane. A chestnut tree in the Tuileries' garden must have been toppled in the 60-mile-an-hour wind. Capitals in the old quarters must have fallen, splitting, killing.

From what point do I interrogate, hearing both shores of the oceans, from what point comes this hurricane, so worthy of credit, so honorable in debt, straight at the hospital windows? Ay the immutable directions that oscillate between the hurricane and this direct effort to cough or defecate. Ay the immutable directions that thus graft death into the innards of the hospitals and wake clandestine cells, so poorly timed, in the cadavers.

What would the sick man, the one asleep right over there, think of himself had he perceived the hurricane? The poor guy sleeps, face up, at the head of his morphine, at the foot of all his sanity. A dram more or less in the dose and they will cart him off to be buried, belly ripped open, face up, deaf to the hurricane, deaf to his ripped belly, over which the doctors are accustomed to debate and ponder at great lengths only to finally pronounce their simple words of men.

La familia rodea al enfermo agrupándose ante sus sienes regresivas, indefensas, sudorosas. Ya no existe hogar sino en torno al velador del pariente enfermo, donde montan guardia impaciente, sus zapatos vacantes, sus cruces de repuesto, sus píldoras de opio. La familia rodea la mesita por espacio de un alto dividendo. Una mujer acomoda en el borde de la mesa, la taza, que casi se ha caído.

¿Ignoro lo que será del enfermo esta mujer, que le besa y no puede sanarle con el beso, le mira y no puede sanarle con los ojos, le habla y no puede sanarle con el verbo? ¿Es su madre? ¿Y cómo, pues, no puede sanarle? ¿Es su amada? ¿Y cómo, pues, no puede sanarle? ¿Es su hermana? ¿Y cómo, pues, no puede sanarle? ¿Es, simplemente, una mujer? ¿Y cómo, pues, no puede sanarle? ¡Por que esta mujer le ha besado, le ha mirado, le ha hablado y hasta le ha cubierto mejor el cuello al enfermo y, cosa verdaderamente asombrosa, no le ha sanado!

El paciente contempla su calzado vacante. Traen queso. Llevan tierra. La muerte se acuesta al pie del lecho, a dormir en sus tranquilas aguas y se duerme. Entonces, los libres pies del hombre enfermo, sin menudencias ni pormenores innecesarios, se estiran en acento circunflejo, y se alejan, en una extensión de dos cuerpos de novios, del corazón.

El cirujano ausculta a los enfermos horas enteras. Hasta donde sus manos cesan de trabajar, y empiezan a jugar, las lleva a tientas, rozando la piel de los pacientes, en tanto sus párpados científicos vibran, tocados por la indocta, por la humana flaqueza del amor. Y he visto a esos enfermos morir precisamente del amor desdoblado del cirujano, de los largos diagnósticos, de las dosis exactas, del riguroso análisis de orinas y excrementos. Se rodeaba de improviso un lecho con un biombo. Médicos y enfermeros cruzaban delante del ausente, pizarra triste y próxima, que un niño llenara de números, en un gran monismo de pálidos miles. Cruzaban así, mirando a

The family surrounds the sick man clustering at his regressive defenseless sweaty temples. A sense of home no longer exists save around the sick relative's night table, where his vacant shoes, his spare crosses, his opium pills impatiently mount guard. The family surrounds the little table for the space of a high dividend. A woman puts back, at the edge of the table, the cup which had almost fallen.

I don't know who this woman is to this sick man, for she kisses him and can't heal him with her kiss, she looks at him and can't heal him with her eyes, she talks to him and can't heal him with her words. Is she his mother? Well then, why can't she heal him? Is she his belovéd? Then why can't she heal him? Is she his sister? Then why can't she heal him? Is she simply a woman? Then why can't she heal him? For this woman has kissed him and has watched over him and has talked to him, even has real carefully covered his neck for him and, the truly astonishing fact is, *she's not healed him*!

The patient contemplates his vacant shoes and socks. They bring cheese. They carry earth. Death lies down at the foot of the bed to sleep in his tranquil waters and does sleep. Then the freed feet of the sick man, without trifles or unnecessary detail, jerk in circumflex accent and pull away, in an extension of two lovers' bodies, from his heart.

The surgeon auscultates the sick for hours on end. When his hands quit working and start playing, he allows them to drift blindly, grazing the patients' skin, while his scientific eyebrows vibrate, played upon by the uncultured and human frailty of love. And I have seen these sick die precisely from the surgeon's spread-open love, from the lengthy diagnoses, from the exact doses, from the rigorous analysis of urine and excrement. Suddenly a bed is encircled with a folding screen. Doctors and orderlies were crossing in front of the absent one, sad and close blackboard that a child had filled with num-

los otros, como si más irreparable fuese morir de apendicitis o neumonía, y no morir al sesgo del paso de los hombres.

Sirviendo la causa de la religión, vuela con éxito esta mosca, a lo largo de la sala. Ciertamente, a la hora de la visita de los cirujanos, sus zumbidos nos perdonan el pecho, pero desarrollándose luego se adueñan del aire, para saludar con genio de mudanza, a los que van a morir. Unos enfermos oyen a esa mosca hasta durante el dolor y de ellos depende, por eso, el linaje del disparo en las noches tremebundas.

¿Cuánto tiempo ha durado la anestesia, que llaman los hombres? ¡Ciencia de Dios, Teodicea! si se me echa a vivir en tales condiciones, anestesiado totalmente, volteada mi sensibilidad para adentro! ¡Ah doctores de las sales, hombres de las esencias, prójimos de las bases! ¡Pido se me deje con mi tumor de conciencia, con mi irritada lepra sensitiva, ocurra lo que ocurra, aunque me muera! Dejadme dolerme, si lo queréis, mas dejadme despierto de sueño, con todo el universo metido, aunque fuese a las malas, en mi temperatura polvorosa.

En el mundo de la salud perfecta, se reirá por esta perspectiva en que padezco, pero, en el mismo plano y cortando la baraja del juego, percute aquí otra risa de contrapunto.

En la casa del dolor, la queja asalta síncopes de gran compositor, golletes de carácter, que nos hacen cosquillas de verdad, atroces, arduas, y, cumpliendo lo prometido, nos hielan de espantosa incertidumbre.

En la casa del dolor, la queja arranca frontera excesiva. No se reconoce en esta queja de dolor, a la propia queja de la dicha en éxtasis, cuando el amor y la carne se eximen de azor y cuando al regresar, hay discordia bastante par el diálogo.

bers in a great monism of chalky thousands. They kept on crossing, looking at the others as if it were more irreparable to die from appendicitis or pneumonia than to die aslant the path of men.

Serving religion's cause this fly sails successfully all around the sickroom. During the surgeons' visiting hours her buzzings undoubtedly absolve our chests, but then increasing to a roar they take over the air to salute in the spirit of change those who are about to die. Some of the sick hear this fly even in their pain and on them depends, and for that reason, the lineage of the gunshot in the dreadful nights.

How long has this named-by-man anesthesia lasted? Science of God, Theodicy, if I'm forced to live under such conditions, totally anesthetized, my sensibility turned toward the inside! Ah doctors of the salts, men of the essences, neighbors of the bases! I'm begging you to leave me with my tumor of consciousness, with my raw sensitive leprosy, no matter what happens, even though I may die! Let me rack myself if you wish, but leave me awake in my dream with all the universe embedded, even though I go through hell, in my dusty temperature.

In the world of perfect health, the perspective on which I suffer will be mocked, but, on the same plane and cutting the deck for the game, another laugh percusses here in counterpoint.

In the house of pain, the cry assaults held notes of the great composer, bottlenecks of character, which give us real chills, arduous atrocious chills, and, fulfilling what is prophesied, freeze us in terrifying uncertainty.

In the house of pain, the cry uproots excessive frontier. The cry itself of happiness in ecstasy, when love and the flesh

¿Dónde está, pues, el otro flanco de esta queja de dolor, si, a estimarla en conjunto, parte ahora del lecho de un hombre?

De la casa del dolor parten quejas tan sordas e inefables y tan colmadas de tanta plenitud, que llorar por ellas sería poco, y sería ya mucho sonreír.

Se atumulta la sangre en el termómetro.

¡No es grato morir, señor, si en la vida nada se deja y si en la muerte nada es posible, sino sobre lo que se deja en la vida!

¡No es grato morir, señor, si en la vida nada se deja y si en la muerte nada es posible, sino sobre lo que se deja en la vida!

¡No es grato morir, señor, si en la vida nada se deja y si en la muerte nada es posible, sino sobre lo que pudo dejarse en la vida.

are exempt from the goshawk and when after union there is enough discord for dialogue, cannot be recognized in this cry of pain.

Then where is the other flank of this cry of pain if, to estimate it as a whole, it breaks now from the bed of a man?

From the house of pain cries break so gagged and ineffable and so brimming and overflowing with so much fullness that to weep for them would be ridiculous and would really be smiling.

Blood in the thermometer rises in arms.

It is not pleasant to die, lord, if nothing is left in life and in death nothing is possible except on the basis of what is left in life.

It is not pleasant to die, lord, if nothing is left in life and in death nothing is possible except on the basis of what is left in life.

It is not pleasant to die, lord, if nothing is left in life and in death nothing is possible except on the basis of what one could have left in life.

Piedra Negra sobre una Piedra Blanca

Me moriré en París con aguacero,
un día del cual tengo y el recuerdo.
Me moriré en París — y no me corro —
talvez un jueves, como es hoy, de otoño.

Jueves será, porque hoy, jueves, que proso
estos versos, los húmeros me he puesto
a la mala y, jamás como hoy, me he vuelto,
con todo mi camino, a verme solo.

César Vallejo ha muerto, le pegaban
todos sin que él les haga nada;
le daban duro con un palo y duro

también con una soga; son testigos
los días jueves y los huesos húmeros,
le soledad, la lluvia, los caminos . . .

Black Stone on a White Stone

I will die in Paris with hard dirty rain,
on a day I now remember.
I will die in Paris – and I don't run –
maybe a Thursday, like today, in autumn.

Thursday, because today, Thursday, when I prose
these lines, I have forced my humeri on
unwillingly and, never like today have I again,
with all my road, seen myself alone.

César Vallejo is dead, they beat him,
everyone, without him doing anything to them;
they hit him hard with a stick and hard

likewise with a rope; witnesses are
the Thursdays and the humerus bones,
the loneliness, the rain, the roads . . .

La vida, esta vida
me placía, su instrumento, esas palomas . . .
Me placía escucharlas gobernarse en lontananza,
advenir naturales, determinado el número,
y ejecutar, según sus aflicciones, sus dianas de animales.

Encogido,
oí desde mis hombros
su sosegada producción,
cabe los albañales sesgar sus trece huesos,
dentro viejo tornillo hincharse el plomo.
Sus paujiles picos,
pareadas palomitas,
las pobridas, hojeándose los hígados,
sobrinas de la nube . . . ¡Vida! ¡Vida! ¡Esta es la vida!

Zurear su tradición rojo les era,
rojo moral, palomas vigilantes,
talvez rojo de herrumbre,
si caían entonces azulmente.

Su elemental cadena,
sus viajes de individuales pájaros viajeros,
echaron humo denso,
pena física, pórtico influyente.

Life, this life
pleased me, its instrument, those doves . . .
Pleased me to hear them steer far away,
turn out natural, settling their number,
and perform, according to their aches, their animal reveilles.

Withdrawn,
I heard from my shoulders
their calm production,
it let the bricklayers slant their thirteen bones,
the lead swell within old screw.
Their cashew beaks,
coupled little doves,
so potrid, rippling their livers,
nephews of the cloud . . .   Life!   Life!   This is life!

To coo their tradition to them was red,
moral red, vigilant doves,
maybe rust red
if they fell then bluely.

Their elemental chain,
their journeys of individual journeying birds,
they mated dense smoke,
physical pain, influential portico.

Palomas saltando, indelebles
palomas olorosas,
manferidas venían, advenían
por azarosas vías digestivas,
a contarme sus cosas fosforosas,
pájaros de contar,
pájaros transitivos y orejones . . .

No escucharé ya más desde mis hombros
huesudo, enfermo, en cama,
ejecutar sus dianas de animales . . . Me doy cuenta.

Bursting ineffaceable doves,
fragrant doves,
handwounded they'd come, would turn up
along hazardous digestive routes
to tell me their phosphorescent things,
storytelling birds,
transitive long-lobed birds . . .

No longer from my shoulders will I hear
bony, sick, in bed,
their animal reveilles performed . . .   I understand.

Hoy me gusta la vida mucho menos,
pero siempre me gusta vivir: ya lo decía.
Casi toqué la parte de mi todo y me contuve
con un tiro en la lengua detrás de mi palabra.

Hoy me palpo el mentón en retirada
y en estos momentáneos pantalones yo me digo:
¡Tánta vida y jamás!
¡Tántos años y siempre mis semanas! . . .
Mis padres enterrados con su piedra
y su triste estirón que no ha acabado;
de cuerpo entero hermanos, mis hermanos,
y, en fin, mi sér parado y en chaleco.

Me gusta la vida enormemente
pero, desde luego,
con mi muerte querida y mi café
y viendo los castaños frondosos de París
y diciendo:
Es un ojo éste, aquél; una frente ésta, aquella . . . Y repitiendo:
¡Tánta vida y jamás me falla la tonada!
¡Tántos años y siempre, siempre, siempre!

Dije chaleco, dije
todo, parte, ansia, dije casi por no llorar.
Que es verdad que sufrí en aquel hospital que queda al lado

Today I like life much less,
but still I like being alive: I knew it.
I almost touched the part of my whole and checked
myself with a shot in the tongue behind my word.

Today I touch my chin in retreat
and in these momentary trousers I tell myself
So much life and never!
So many years and always my weeks!
My parents buried with their stone
and their sad death-jerk that's not ended;
completely portrayed brothers, my brothers,
in short, my béing erect in a vest.

I like life enormously
but, after all,
with my beloved death and my coffee
and seeing the leafy chestnuts of Paris
and saying: this is an eye, and that one; this is a forehead, and
that one . . . And repeating:
So much life and the tune never fails me!
So many years and always always always!

I said vest, said
whole, part, anxiety, said almost by not weeping.
For it's true I suffered in that hospital next door

y está bien y está mal haber mirado
de abajo para arriba mi organismo.

Me gustará vivir siempre, así fuese de barriga,
porque, como iba diciendo y lo repito,
¡tánta vida y jamás! ¡Y tantos años,
y siempre, mucho siempre, siempre, siempre!

and it's good and it's bad to have watched
from below up my organism.

I'd like to live always, even flat on my belly,
because as I was saying and I say it again
So much life and never! And so many years,
and always, much always, always always!

Hallazgo de la Vida

¡Señores! Hoy es la primera vez que me doy cuenta de la presencia de la vida. ¡Señores! Ruego a ustedes dejarme libre un momento, para saborear esta emoción formidable, espontánea y reciente de la vida, que hoy, por la primera vez, me extasía y me hace dichoso hasta las lágrimas.

Mi gozo viene de lo inédito de mi emoción. Mi exultación viene de que antes no sentí la presencia de la vida. No la he sentido nunca. Miente quien diga que la he sentido. Miente y su mentira me hiere a tal punto que me haría desgraciado. Mi gozo viene de mi fe en este hallazgo personal de la vida, y nadie puede ir contra esa fe. Al que fuera, se le caería la lengua, se le caerían los huesos y correría el peligro de recoger otros, ajenos, para mantenerse de pie ante mis ojos.

Nunca, sino ahora, ha habido vida. Nunca, sino ahora, han pasado gentes. Nunca, sino ahora, ha habido casas y avenidas, aire y horizontes. Si viniese ahora mi amigo Peyriet, le diría que yo no le conozco y que debemos empezar de nuevo. ¿Cuando, en efecto, le he conocido a mi amigo Peyriet? Hoy sería la primera vez que nos conocemos. Le diría que se vaya y regrese y entre a verme, como si no me conociera, es decir, por la primera vez.

Ahora yo no conozco a nadie ni nada. Me advierto en un país extraño, en el que todo cobra relieve de nacimiento, luz

Discovery of Life

Gentlemen! Today is the first time that I realize the presence of life! Gentlemen! I beg you leave me alone for a moment so I can savor this marvelous, spontaneous, new-life emotion, that today for the first time enraptures me and makes me so happy I'm crying.

My joy comes from what is unpublished of my emotion. My exultation comes from not feeling before the presence of life. I've never felt it. He lies who says I've felt it. He lies, and his lie probes me so deep that it would make me miserable. My joy comes from my faith in this personal discovery of life, and no one can oppose this faith. No matter who he was, his tongue would fall out, his bones would fall out, and he'd risk picking up others, not his own, to keep himself up before my eyes.

Never, until now, has life been. Never, until now, have people walked by. Never, until now, have there been houses and avenues, air and horizon. If my friend Peyriet came over right now, I'd tell him I don't know him, that we must begin anew. When in fact háve I known my friend Peyriet? Today would be the first time we became acquainted. I'd tell him to go away and come back, to drop in on me, as if he didn't know me, that is, for the first time.

Now I know no one, nothing. I observe myself in a foreign country where everything appears in birth relief, light

de epifanía inmarcesible. No, señor. No hable usted a ese caballero. Usted no lo conoce y le sorprendería tan inopinada parla. No ponga usted el pie sobre esa piedrecilla: quien sabe no es piedra y vaya usted a dar en el vacío. Sea usted precavido, puesto que estamos en un mundo absolutamente inconocido.

¡Cuán poco tiempo he vivido! Mi nacimiento es tan reciente, que no hay unidad de medida para contar mi edad. ¡Si acabo de nacer! ¡Si aún no he vivido todavía! Señores: soy tan pequeñito, que el día apenas cabe en mí.

Nunca, sino ahora, oí el estruendo de los carros, que cargan piedras para una gran construcción del boulevard Haussmann. Nunca, sino ahora, avancé paralelamente a la primavera, diciéndola: "Si la muerte hubiera sido otra . . ." Nunca, sino ahora, vi la luz áurea del sol sobre las cúpulas del Sacré-Coeur. Nunca, sino ahora, se me acercó un niño y me miró hondamente con su boca. Nunca, sino ahora, supe que existía una puerta, otra puerta y el canto cordial de las distancias.

¡Dejadme! La vida me ha dado ahora en toda mi muerte.

of unfading epiphany. No, sir. Don't even speak to that gentleman. You don't know him and such careless chatter would surprise him. Don't put your foot on that little stone; maybe it's not a stone and you'll plunge into the void. Be cautious; we're in a totally unknown world.

How short I've lived! My birth is so recent there's no unit of measure to tell my age. Why I've just been born! Why I've not lived yet! Gentlemen: I'm so tiny the day hardly fits in me.

Never, until now, did I hear the carts' clatter carrying rock for the broad Haussmann Boulevard. Never, until now, did I advance parallel with the spring, addressing it: "If death had only been something else . . ." Never, until now, did I see the aureate light of the sun on the cupolas of Sacré-Coeur. Never, until now, did a child approach me and look so deeply into me with his mouth. Never, until now, did I know a door existed, another door and the cordial song of the distances.

Let me alone! Life has struck me today square in my death!

Telúrica y Magnética

¡Mecánica sincera y peruanísima
la del cerro colorado!
¡Suelo teórico y práctico!
¡Surcos inteligentes; ejemplo: el monolito y su cortejo!
¡Papales, cebadales, alfalfares, cosa buena!
¡Cultivos que integra una asombrosa jerarquía de útiles
y que integran con viento los mujidos,
las aguas con su sorda antigüedad!

¡Cuaternarios maíces, de opuestos natalicios,
los oigo por los pies cómo se alejan,
los huelo retornar cuando la tierra
tropieza con la técnica del cielo!
¡Molécula ex abrupto! Atomo terso!

¡Oh campos humanos!
¡Solar y nutricia ausencia de la mar,
y sentimiento oceánico de todo!
¡Oh climas encontrados dentro del oro, listos!
¡Oh campo intelectual de cordillera,
con religión, con campo, con patitos!
¡Paquidermos en prosa cuando pasan
y en verso cuando páranse!
¡Roedores que miran con sentimiento judicial en torno!
¡Oh patrióticos asnos de mi vida!
¡Vicuña, descendiente nacional y graciosa de mi mono!

Telluric and Magnetic

Sincere and very Peruvian mechanics
our lady of the red-rutted hill!
Ground theoretical *and* practical!
Intelligent furrows; for instance: the monolith and his court!
Potatofields barleyfields lucernefields, great!
Cultivations that integrate an astonishing hierarchy of tools,
that integrate with wind the lowings,
the waters with their deaf antiquity!

Quaternary maize from opposite births
I hear through my feet how you withdraw,
I smell you return when earth comes
up against the technique of sky!
Crazed molecule! Terse atom! O

h u m a n f i e l d s !
Sunswept nutritious absence of the sea,
oceanic sentiment about everything!
O climates met inside gold, kinetic!
O intellectual field of cordillera
with religion, with country, with baby ducks!
Pachyderms in prose when they pass
poetry when they halt!
Rodents peering with judicial feeling all around!
O patriotic asses of my life!
Vicuña, national and graceful descendant of my ape!

¡Oh luz que dista apenas un espejo de la sombra,
que es vida con el punto y, con la línea, polvo
y que por eso acato, subiendo por la idea a mi osamenta!

¡Siega en época de dilatado molle,
del farol que colgaron de la sien
y del que descolgaron de la barreta espléndida!
¡Angeles de corral,
aves por un descuido de la cresta!
Cuya o cuy para comerlos fritos
con el bravo rocoto de los templos!
(¿Cóndores? ¡Me friegan los cóndores!)
Leños cristianos en gracia
al tronco feliz y al tallo competente!
¡Familiar de los líquenes,
especies en basáltica formación que yo
respeto
desde este modestísimo papel!
¡Cuatro operaciones, os sustraigo
para salvar al roble y hundirlo en buena ley!
¡Cuestas en fraganti!
¡Auquénidos llorosos, almas mías!
¡Sierra de mi Perú, Perú del mundo,
y Perú al pie del orbe; yo me adhiero!
¡Estrellas matutinas si os aromo
quemando hojas de coca en este cráneo,
y cenitales, si destapo,
de un solo sombrerazo, mis diez templos!
¡Brazo de siembra, bájate, y a pie!
Lluvia a base del mediodía,
bajo el techo de tejas donde muerde
la infatigable altura
y la tórtola corta en tres su trino.
Rotación de tardes modernas
y finas madrugadas arquelológicas.
¡Indio después del hombre y antes de él!

O light hardly a mirror distant from the shadow
that is life with the point and in lineage dust
and for this I bow, rising through the idea to my skeleton!

Harvest in season of the dilated peppertree,
of the lantern they held up to a man's temple
and of the one they unhooked from that magnificent bar!
Cooped angels,
birds by the slip of a cockscomb!
Guinea-pigess or -pig to be eaten fried
with the burning tomato pepper of the temples!
(Condors? I'm fed up with these fucking condors!)
Christian logs by the grace
of a happy trunk and competent branch!
Relative of the lichen,
species in basalt formation that I
respect
from this most modest paper!
Reading writing arithmetic, I subtract you out
to save the blockhead and plant him straight!
You're worth in flagrante!
Wet-eyed auchenia, souls of my soul!
Sierra of my Peru, Peru of the world
and Peru at the foot of the earth; I stick!
Morning stars if I perfume you
burning coca leaves in this skull,
zeniths if I unveil
with a single doff my ten temples!
Arm made for sowing, get down, and on foot!
Rain based on noon
under the tile roof where indefatigable
altitude gnaws
and the turtledove files in threes her trill.
Rotation of modern evenings
and delicate archaeological dawns.
Indian after man and before him!

¡Lo entiendo todo en dos flautas
y me doy a entender en una quena!
¡Y los demás, me las pelan! . . .

I understand it all on two flutes
and I make myself understood on a quena!
The rest they peel off my balls! . . .

¡Dulzura por dulzura corazona!
Dulzura a gajos, eras de vista,
esos abiertos días, cuando monté por árboles caídos!
Así por tu paloma palomita,
por tu oración pasiva,
andando entre tu sombra y el gran tesón corpóreo de tu
sombra.

Debajo de ti y yo,
tú y yo, sinceramente,
tu candado ahogándose de llaves,
yo ascendiendo y sudando
y haciendo lo infinito entre tus muslos.
(El hotelero es una bestia,
sus dientes, admirables; yo controlo
el orden pálido de mi alma:
señor, allá distante . . . paso paso . . . adiós, señor . . .)

Mucho pienso en todo esto conmovido, perduroso
y pongo tu paloma a la altura de tu vuelo
y, cojeando de dicha, a veces,
repósome a la sombra de ese árbol arrastrado.

Costilla de mi cosa,
dulzura que tú tapas sonriendo con tu mano;
tu traje negro que se habrá acabado,

Sweetness through heartic sweetness!
Sweetness cluster by cluster, you were by sight
those open days when I mounted along fallen trees!
Thus through your little dove dove,
through your passive sentence,
strolling between your shadow and your shadow's great corporeal firmness.

Under you and I,
you and I, sincerely,
your padlock choking with keys,
me climbing and sweating
and making what is infinite between your thighs.
(The hotel manager is an idiot,
admirable teeth; I check
what's left of my soul order:
way over there, mister . . . go on, go on . . . goodbye, mister . . .)

I think so much about all this moved, I never let go
and put your dove at the height of your flight
and, limping with happiness, at times,
I repose in the shadow of this dragged-on tree.

Rib of my thing,
sweetness you cover smiling with your hand,
your black dress that by now must be worn out,

amada, amada en masa,
¡qué unido a tu rodilla enferma!

Simple ahora te veo, te comprendo avergonzado
en Letonia, Alemania, Rusia, Bélgica, tu ausente,
tu portátil ausente,
hombre convulso de la mujer temblando entre sus vínculos.

¡Amada en la figura de tu cola irreparable,
amada que yo amara con fósforos floridos,
quand on a la vie et la jeunesse,
c'est déjà tellement!

Cuando ya no haya espacio
entre tu grandeza y mi postrer proyecto,
amada,
volveré a tu media, has de besarme,
bajando por tu media repetida,
tu portátil ausente, dile así . . .

[*Hacia 1937*]

belovéd, belovéd in mass,
how bound to your sick knee!

Simple I see you now, I understand you ashamed in
Lithuania, Germany, Russia, Belgium, your absent one,
your portable absent one,
man convulsed from the woman trembling between his bind-
ings.

Belovéd in the figure of your irreparable tail,
belovéd who I used to love with florescent matches,
quand on a la vie et la jeunesse,
c'est déjà tellement!

When there's no longer space
between your greatness and my last project
belovéd,
I'll come back to your stocking, you will kiss me,
going down along your repeated stocking,
your portable absent one, tell him like this . . .

The Dated Poems

[4 September–8 December, 1937]

Calor, cansado voy con mi oro, a donde
acaba mi enemigo de quererme.
¡C'est Septembre attiédi, por ti, Febrero!
Es como si me hubieran puesto aretes.

París, y 4, y 5, y la ansiedad
colgada, en el calor, de mi hecho muerto.
¡C'est Paris reine du monde!
Es como si se hubieran orinado.

Hojas amargas de mensual tamaño
y hojas del Luxemburgo polvorosas.
¡C'est l'été, por ti, invierno de alta pleura!
Es como si se hubieran dado vuelta.

Calor, París, otoño, ¡cuánto estío
en medio del calor y de la urbe!
¡C'est la vie, mort de la Mort!
Es como si contaran mis pisadas.

¡Es como si me hubieran puesto aretes!
¡Es como si se hubieran orinado!
¡Es como si te hubieras dado vuelta!
¡Es como si contaran mis pisadas!

4 septiembre 1937

Heat, tired I go with my gold to where
my enemy quits loving me.
C'est Septembre attiédi, for you, February!
It's as if they'd hung me with earrings.

Paris, and the 4th, and the 5th, and the anxiety
pendant, in the heat, on my dead fact.
C'est Paris reine du monde!
It's as if they'd urinated on themselves.

Bitter leaves of monthly proportion
and dusty leaves of the Luxembourg.
C'est l'été, for you, winter of high pleura!
It's as if they'd turned around.

Heat, Paris, autumn, so much summer
in the midst of the heat and the metropolis!
C'est la vie, mort de la Mort!
It's as if they counted my steps.

It's as if they'd hung me with earrings!
As if they'd urinated on themselves!
As if you'd turned around!
As if they counted my steps!

Un pilar soportando consuelos,
pilar otro,
pilar en duplicado, pilaroso
y como nieto de una puerta oscura.
Ruido perdido, el uno, oyendo, al borde del cansancio;
bebiendo, el otro, dos a dos, con asas.

¿Ignoro acaso el año de este día,
el odio de este amor, las tablas de esta frente?
¿Ignoro que esta tarde cuesta días?
¿Ignoro que jamás se dice "nunca," de rodillas?

Los pilares que ví me están oyendo;
otros pilares son, doses y nietos tristes de mi pierna.
¡Lo digo en cobre americano,
que le bebe a la plata tánto fuego!

Consolado en terceras nupcias,
pálido, nacido,
voy a cerrar mi pila bautismal, esta vidriera,
este susto con tetas,
este dedo en capilla,
corazonmente unido a mi esqueleto.

6 septiembre 1937

A pillar supporting solace,
pillar other,
duplicate pillar, pillarish
and like the grandchild of a dark door.
Lost noise, the one, listening, at the edge of fatigue;
the other, drinking, two by two, with handles.

I'm ignorant maybe of the year of this day,
the hate of this love, the tablas of this forehead?
Ignorant that this evening costs days?
Ignorant that never does one say "never" on one's knees?

The pillars I saw are listening to me;
other pillars they are, twos and sad grandchildren of my leg.
I say it in American copper
which draws from silver só much fire!

Solaced in third marriage,
pale, born,
I'm going to close my font, this showcase,
this fright with tits,
this enshrined finger,
heartwise tied to my skeleton.

Poema para Ser Leído y Cantado

Sé que hay una persona
que me busca en su mano, día y noche,
encontrándome, a cada minuto, en su calzado.
¿Ignora que la noche está enterrada
con espuelas detrás de la cocina?

Sé que hay una persona compuesta de mis partes,
a la que integro cuando va mi talle
cabalgando en su exacta piedrecilla.
¿Ignora que a su cofre
no volverá moneda que salió con su retrato?

Sé el día,
pero el sol se me ha escapado;
sé el acto universal que hizo en su cama
con ajeno valor y esa agua tibia, cuya
superficial frecuencia es una mina.
¿Tan pequeña es, acaso, esa persona,
que hasta sus propios pies así la pisan?

Un gato es el lindero entre ella y yo,
al lado mismo de su taza de agua.
La veo en las esquinas, se abre y cierra
su veste, antes palmera interrogante . . .
¿Qué podrá hacer sino cambiar de llanto?

Poem to Be Read and Sung

I know there's a person
who looks for me in her hand day and night,
finding me each minute in her shoes.
Doesn't she know the night's buried
with spurs behind the kitchen?

I know there's a person composed of my parts
who I complete when my form
rides off on its exact little stone.
Doesn't she know that the money spent
on her portrait will not return to her trunk?

I know the day
but the sun's escaped me;
I know the universal act she did in her bed
with a courage not her own and that tepid water, whose
superficial frequency is a mine.
Is that person perhaps so small
even her own feet trample her?

A cat is the boundary between her and me,
right at the side of its water bowl.
I see her on the corners, her jacket
opens and closes, actually an interrogative palm tree . . .
What can she do but change weeping?

Pero me busca y busca. ¡Es una historia!

7 septiembre 1937

But she looks and looks for me. What a fucking story!

Al cavilar en la vida, al cavilar
despacio en el esfuerzo del torrente,
alivia, ofrece asiento el existir,
condena a muerte;
envuelto en trapos blancos cae,
cae planetariamente,
el clavo hervido en pesadumbre; ¡cae!
(Actitud oficial, la de mi izquierda;
viejo bolsillo, en sí considerada esta derecha.)

¡Todo está alegre, menos mi alegría
y todo, largo, menos mi candor,
mi incertidumbre!
A juzgar por la forma, no obstante, voy de frente,
cojeando antiguamente,
y olvido por mis lágrimas mis ojos (Muy interesante)
y subo hasta mis pies desde mi estrella.

Tejo; de haber hilado, héme tejiendo.
Busco lo que me sigue y se me esconde entre arzobispos,
por debajo de mi alma y tras del humo de mi aliento.
Tal era la sensual desolación
de la cabra doncella que ascendía,
exhalando petróleos fatídicos,
ayer domingo en que perdí mi sábado.

Brooding on life, brooding
slowly on the strength of the torrent,
existence eases, gives ground,
condemns to death;
wrapped in white rags it falls,
falls planetarily,
the nail boiled in grief; falls!
(Official attitude, that of my left;
old pocket, in itself this right considered.)

Everything is joyful, minus my joy
and everything, long, minus my candor,
my incertitude!
To judge by the form nonetheless I go facing,
limping antiquely,
and forget for my tears my eyes (Very interesting)
and rise to my feet from my star.

I knit; having woven, I'm knitting myself in.
I search for what follows me and hides from me between archbishops,
under my soul and behind the smoke of my breathing.
Such was the sensual desolation
of the virgin goat that ascended
exhaling ominous petroleums,
yesterday Sunday on which I lost my Saturday.

Tal es la muerte, con su audaz marido.

7 septiembre 1937

Such is death, with her daring husband.

El acento me pende del zapato;
le oigo perfectamente
sucumbir, lucir, doblarse en forma de ámbar
y colgar, colorante, mala sombra.
Me sobra así el tamaño,
me ven jueces desde un árbol,
me ven con sus espaldas ir de frente,
entrar a mi martillo,
pararme a ver a una niña
y, al pie de un urinario, alzar los hombros.

Seguramente nadie está a mi lado,
me importa poco, no lo necesito;
seguramente han dicho que me vaya:
lo siento claramente.

¡Cruelísimo tamaño el de rezar!
¡Humillación, fulgor, profunda selva!
Me sobra ya tamaño, bruma elástica,
rapidez por encima y desde y junto.
¡Imperturbable! ¡Imperturbable! Suenan
luego, después, fatídicos teléfonos.
Es el acento; es él.

12 septiembre 1937

The accent hangs from my shoe;
I hear it succumb
perfectly, shine, fold in the shape of amber
and hang, colorish, evil shade.
I'm thus too big for myself,
judges see me from a tree,
they see me with their backs walk forward,
enter my hammer,
stop to look at a little girl
and, at the foot of a urinal, shrug my shoulders.

Of course no one's with me,
I don't much care, don't need it;
of course they've told me to be off:
I feel it clearly.

The cruelest size is praying!
Humiliation, radiance, endless jungle!
I'm now too big for myself, elastic mist,
velocity from above and as soon as and at hand.
Imperturbable! Imperturbable! They ring
later, afterward, prophetic telephones.
It's the accent; it's him.

La punto del hombre,
el ludibrio pequeño de encojerse
tras de fumar su universal ceniza;
punta al darse en secretos caracoles,
punta donde se agarra uno con guantes,
punta el lunes sujeta por seis frenos,
punta saliendo de escuchar a su alma.

De otra manera,
fueran lluvia menuda los soldados
y ni cuadrada pólvora, al volver de los bravos desatinos,
y ni letales plátanos; tan sólo
un poco de patilla en la silueta.
De otra manera, caminantes suegros,
cuñados en misión sonora,
yernos por la vía ingratísima del jebe,
toda la gracia caballar andando
puede fulgir esplendorosamente!

¡Oh pensar geométrico al trasluz!
¡Oh no morir bajamente
de majestad tan rauda y tan fragante!
¡Oh no cantar; apenas
escribir y escribir con un palito
o con el filo de la oreja inquieta!

The point of the man,
the ignoble mockery of shrinking
after smoking his universal ash;
point striking into secret snails,
point one grabs with gloves on,
point Monday holds back with six brakes,
point inching out to listen to its soul.

On the other hand,
the soldiers would be a fine rain
and not even gunpowder squared, returning from their fierce
blunders,
and not even lethal bananas; only
a little sideburn on the silhouette.
On the other hand, wandering fathers-in-law,
brothers-in-law on a noisy mission,
sons-in-law down the thankless bin of a rubber,
all the equine grace walking
can flash a thousand suns!

O geometrical thought against the light!
O not to die lowly
of majesty so swift and so fragrant!
O not to sing; to barely
write and write with a little stick
or with the edge of one's restless ear!

Acorde de lápiz, tímpano sordísimo,
dondoneo en mitades robustas
y comer de memoria buena carne,
jamón, si falta carne,
y un pedazo de queso con gusanos hembras,
gusanos machos y gusanos muertos.

14 septiembre 1937

Pencil chord, most deaf eardrum,
dudududum in robust halves
and to eat from memory a nice piece of ass,
hamhock, if there's no ass,
and a wedge of cheese full of female worms,
male worms dead worms.

¡Oh botella sin vino! ¡oh vino que enviudó de esta botella!
Tarde cuando la aurora de la tarde
flameó funestamente en cinco espíritus.
Viudez sin pan ni mugre, rematando en horrendos metaloides
y en células orales acabando.

¡Oh siempre, nunca dar con el jamás de tanto siempre!
¡Oh mis buenos amigos, cruel falacia,
parcial, penetrativa en nuestro trunco,
volátil, jugarino desconsuelo!

¡Sublime, baja perfección del cerdo,
palpa mi general melancolía!
¡Zuela sonante en sueños,
zuela
zafia, inferior, vendida, lícita, ladrona,
baja y palpa lo que eran mis ideas!

Tú y él y ellos y todos,
sin embargo,
entraron a la vez en mi camisa,
en los hombros madera, entre los fémures, palillos;
tú particularmente,
habiéndome influído;

O bottle without wine! O wine that widowed from this bottle!
Late when the aurora of evening
flamed forebodingly in five spirits.
Widowhood without bread or grease, closing in horrendous metalloids
and in oral cells ending.

O always, never to find the never of so much always!
O my good friends, cruel deceit,
partial, cutting into our cut-
short volatile playful grief!

Sublime base pig perfection
palpates my general melancholy!
Zole sounding in dreams,
gross inferior betrayer licit thief
zole, lower!
feel what were my ideas!

You and he and they and everyone,
nevertheless,
entered my shirt all at once,
in my shoulders, wood, between my femurs, little sticks;
you particularly,
having influenced me;

él, fútil, colorado, con dinero
y ellos, zánganos de ala de otro peso.

¡Oh botella sin vino! ¡oh vino que enviudó de esta botella!

16 septiembre 1937

he, futile, loaded, flushed
and they, drones decked out in others' wings.

O bottle without wine! O wine that widowed from this bottle!

Va corriendo, andando, huyendo
de sus pies . . .
Va con dos nubes en su nube,
sentado apócrifo, en la mano insertos
sus tristes paras, sus entonces fúnebres.

Corre de todo, andando
entre protestas incoloras; huye
subiendo, huye
bajando, huye
a paso de sotana, huye
alzando al mal en brazos,
huye
directamente a sollozar a solas.

Adonde vaya,
lejos de sus fragosos, cáusticos talones,
lejos del aire, lejos de su viaje,
a fin de huir, huir y huir y huir
de sus pies — hombre en dos pies, parado
de tánto huir — habrá sed de correr.

¡Y ni el árbol, si endosa hierro de oro!
¡Y ni el hierro, si cubre su hojarasca!

He is running, walking, fleeing
from his feet . . .
Running with two clouds on his cloud,
apocryphal seated, his funereal thens
his sad in-order-tos inserted in his hand.

He runs from everything, walking
between colorless protests; he flees
rising, flees
lowering, flees
at the step of a cassock, flees
raising the evil in his arms,
flees
directly to sob alone.

Wherever he goes,
far from his rough caustic heels,
far from the air, far from his journey,
at last to flee, to flee and to flee and to flee
from his feet – man on both feet, standing
from so much flight – will have a thirst for running.

And not the tree, if it endorses iron with gold!
And not the iron, if it hides dead foliage!

Nada, sino sus pies,
nada sino su breve calofrío,
sus paras vivos, sus entonces vivos . . .

18 septiembre 1937

Nothing, except his feet,
nothing except his brief chill,
his alive in-order-tos, his alive thens . . .

Al fin, un monte
detrás de la bajura: al fin, humeante nimbo
alrededor, durante un rostro fijo.

Monte en honor del pozo,
sobre filones de gratuita plata de oro.

Es la franja a que arrástranse,
seguras de sus tonos de verano,
las que eran largas válvulas difuntas;
el taciturno marco de este arranque
natural, de este augusto zapatazo,
de esta piel, de este intrínseco destello
digital, en que estoy entero, lúbrico.

Quehaceres en un pie, mecha de azufre,
oro de plata y plata hecha de plata
y mi muerte, mi hondura, mi colina.

¡Pasar
abrazado a mis brazos,
destaparme después o antes del corcho!
Monte que tantas veces manara
oración, prosa fluvial de llanas lágrimas;
monte bajo, compuesto de suplicantes gradas
y, más allá, de torrenciales torres;

Finally, a mountain
after the lowland: finally, smoking halo
around, during an unchanging face.

Mountain in honor of the well
over veins of free silver of gold.

It's the fringe toward which drag
sure with their summer tones
those who were defunct long valves;
the tacit frame of this natural
start, of this august shoe-smack,
of this skin, of this intrinsic digital
gleam in which I am lubricated, whole.

Jobs on one foot, fuse of sulphur,
gold of silver and silver made of silver
and my death, my depth, my hill.

To pass
clasped in my arms,
to uncork me after or before the cork!
Mountain that so often flowed
prayer, fluvial prose of smoothed out tears;
low mountain, of supplicant terraces composed
and, beyond, of torrential towers;

niebla entre el día y el alcohol del día,
caro verdor de coles, tibios asnos
complementarios, palos y maderas;
filones de gratuita plata de oro.

19 septiembre 1937

fog between the day and the alcohol of day,
dear cabbage verdure, indifferent
complementary asses, sticks and woods;
veins of free silver of gold.

Quiere y no quiere su color mi pecho,
por cuyas bruscas vías voy, lloro con palo,
trato de ser feliz, lloro en mi mano,
recuerdo, escribo
y remacho una lágrima en mi pómulo.

Quiere su rojo el mal, el bien su rojo enrojecido
por el hacha suspensa,
por el trote del ala a pie volando,
y no quiere y sensiblemente
no quiere aquesto el hombre;
no quiere estar en su alma
acostado, en la sien latidos de asta,
el bimano, el muy bruto, el muy filósofo.

Así, casi no soy, me vengo abajo
desde el arado en que socorro a mi alma
y casi, en proporción, casi enaltézcome.
Que saber por qué tiene la vida este perrazo
por qué lloro, por qué,
cejón, inhábil, veleidoso, hube nacido
gritando;
saberlo, comprenderlo
al son de un alfabeto competente,
sería padecer por un ingrato.

My chest wants and doesn't want its color,
by whose mountainous roads I force on, weeping with stick,
I try to be happy, I cry in my hand,
remember, write,
and tighten a tear in my cheekbone.

Evil wants its redness, good its redness reddened
by the ax suspended,
by the trot of the wing on foot flying,
and man doesn't want, sensitively
doesn't want that;
he doesn't want to be lying down
in his soul, throbs like horns in his temples,
the two-handed, the damned brute, the damned philosopher.

Thus almost I'm not, I fail
behind the plow on which I aid my soul
and almost, in proportion I, almost exalt myself.
To know why life has this huge dog,
why I weep, why
scowling, helpless, giddy, I was born
shrieking;
to know this, to comprehend it
set to adequate language,
would be to suffer for an ingrate.

¡Y no! ¡No! ¡No! ¡Qué ardid, ni paramento!
Congoja, sí, con sí firme y frenético,
coriáceo, rapaz, quiere y no quiere, cielo y pájaro;
congoja, sí, con toda la bragueta.
Contienda entre dos llantos, robo de una sola ventura,
vía indolora en que padezco en chanclos
de la velocidad de andar a ciegas.

22 septiembre 1937

And no! No! No! What a trick, not even an ornament!

It's anguish, yes, a firm and frantic yes,
coriaceous, rapacious, want and don't want, sky and bird;
anguish, yes, my fly at full gape.
Struggle between two sobs, theft from only one future,
painless road on which I endure in galoshes
the velocity of walking blind.

Esto
sucedió entre dos párpados; temblé
en mi vaina, colérico, alcalino,
parado junto al lúbrico equinoccio,
al pie del frío incendio en que me acabo.

Resbalón alcalino, voy diciendo,
más acá de los ajos, sobre el sentido almíbar,
más adentro, muy más, de las herrumbres,
al ir el agua y al volver la ola.
Resbalón alcalino
también y grandemente, en el montaje colosal del cielo.

¡Qué venablos y arpones lanzaré, si muero
en mi vaina; daré en hojas de plátano sagrado
mis cinco huesecillos subalternos,
y en la mirada, la mirada misma!
(Dicen que en los suspiros se edifican
entonces acordeones óseos, táctiles;
dicen que cuando mueren así los que se acaban,
¡ay! mueren fuera del reloj, la mano
agarrada a un zapato solitario.)

Comprendiéndolo y todo, coronel
y todo, en el sentido llorante de esta voz,
me hago doler yo mismo, extraigo tristemente,

This
happened between two eyelids; I quivered
in my pod, furious, alkaline,
pulled up at the lubricated equinox,
at foot of the cold blaze in which I fizzle out.

Alkaline slip-up I keep saying,
nearer than garlic, over the syrup sense,
deeper in, very more, the rusts,
on going the water and on coming the wave.
Alkaline slip-up
too, a wild one, in the colossal staging of the sky.

What curses and harpoons I'll hurl if I die
in my pod; I'll offer up in sacred banana leaves
my five subaltern little bones,
and in the glance, the glance itself!
(They say that in sighs one builds
then bony tactile accordions;
they say that when those who fizzle out die thus
aie! they die outside the clock, hand
clutching a single shoe.)

Getting it and all, cyma
and all, in the crying sense of this voice,
I make myself suffer, I extract sadly

por la noche, mis uñas;
luego no tengo nada y hablo solo,
reviso mis semestres
y para henchir mi vértebra, me toco.

23 septiembre 1937

at night my fingernails;
then I have nothing and talk alone,
I revise my half-years
and in order to stuff my vertebra, touch.

Quédeme a calentar la tinta en que me ahogo
y a escuchar mi caverna alternativa,
noches de tacto, días de abstracción.

Se estremeció la incógnita en mi amígdala
y crují de una anual melancolía,
noches de sol, días de luna, ocasos de París.

Y todavía, hoy mismo, al atardecer,
digiero sacratísimas constancias,
noches de madre, días de biznieta
bicolor, voluptuosa, urgente, linda.

Y aún
alcanzo, llego hasta mí en avión de dos asientos,
bajo la mañana doméstica y la bruma
que emergió eternamente de un instante.

Y todavía,
aún ahora,
al cabo del cometa en que he ganado
mi bacilo feliz y doctoral,
he aquí que caliente, oyente, tierro, sol y luno,
incógnito atravieso el cementerio,
tomo a la izquierda, hiendo

I stayed on to warm up the ink in which I drown
and to listen to my alternative cavern,
tactile nights, abstracted days.

The unknown quaked in my tonsil
and I creaked from an annual melancholy,
sunlit nights, moonlit days, Parisian sundowns.

And still, this very day, at nightfall,
I digest very sacred constancies,
mother nights, pretty urgent voluptuous
two-colored great-granddaughter days.

And still
I catch up, I reach myself in a plane with two seats
under the domestic morning and the mist
that emerged eternally from an instant.

And still,
even now,
at the tail of the kite where I've won
my happy doctoral bacillus,
it's here that warm, hearer, male-earth, sun, male-moon,
unknown I cross the cemetery,
I cut off to the left, haying

la yerba con un par de endecasílabos,
años de tumba, litros de infinito,
tinta, pluma, ladrillos y perdones.

24 septiembre 1937

the grass with a pair of hendecasyllables,
tomb years, infinity liters,
ink, quill, bricks and forgivenesses.

La paz, la avispa, el taco, las vertientes,
el muerto, los decílitros, el buho,
los lugares, la tiña, los sarcófagos, el vaso, las morenas,
el desconocimiento, la olla, el monaguillo,
las gotas, el olvido,
la potestad, los primos, los arcángeles, la aguja,
los párrocos, el ébano, el desaire,
la parte, el tipo, el estupor, el alma . . .

Dúctil, azafranado, externo, nítido,
portátil, viejo, trece, ensangrentado,
fotografiadas, listas, tumefactas,
conexas, largas, encintadas, pérfidas . . .

Ardiendo, comparando,
viviendo, enfureciéndose,
golpeando, analizando, oyendo, estremeciéndose,
muriendo, sosteniéndose, situándose, llorando . . .

Después, éstos, aquí,
después, encima,
quizá, mientras, detrás, tanto, tan nunca,
debajo, acaso, lejos,
siempre, aquello, mañana, cuánto,
¡cuánto! . . .

Peace, wasp, wad, rivercourse,
corpse, deciliters, owl,
sites, ringworm, sarcophagi, waterglass, brunettes,
ignorance, pot, altarboy,
drops, forgetfulness,
potentate, cousins, archangels, needle,
vicars, ebony, spite,
part, type, stupor, soul . . .

Ductile, saffroned, external, clear,
portable, old, thirteen, bloodsmeared,
they're photographed, ready, tumescent,
they're linked, long, bedecked, perfidious . . .

Burning, comparing,
living, getting infuriated,
striking, analyzing, hearing, shuddering,
dying, holding on, locating, weeping . . .

After, these, here,
after, overhead,
perhaps, while, behind, so much, so never,
beneath, maybe, far,
always, that one, tomorrow, how much,
how much! . . .

Lo horrible, lo suntuario, lo lentísimo,
lo augusto, lo infructuoso,
lo aciago, lo crispante, lo mojado, lo fatal,
lo todo, lo purísimo, lo lóbrego,
lo acerbo, lo satánico, lo táctil, lo profundo . . .

25 septiembre 1937

What is horrible, sumptuous, slowest,
what is august, fruitless,
what is ominous, twitching, wet, fatal,
what is all, purest, lugubrious,
what is tart, satanic, tactile, profound . . .

Transido, salomónico, decente,
ululaba; compuesto, caviloso, cadavérico, perjuro,
iba, tornaba, respondía; osaba,
fatídico, escarlata, irresistible.

En sociedad, en vidrio, en polvo, en hulla,
marchóse; vaciló, en hablando en oro; fulguró,
volteó, en acatamiento;
en terciopelo, en llanto, replegóse.

¿Recordar? ¿Insistir? ¿Ir? ¿Perdonar?
Ceñudo, acabaría
recostado, áspero, atónito, mural;
meditaba estamparse, confundirse, fenecer.

Inatacablemente, impunemente,
negramente, husmeará, comprenderá;
vestiráse oralmente;
inciertamente irá, acobardaráse, olvidará.

26 septiembre 1937

Starved with pain, solomonic, proper,
he was howling; circumspect, over-suspicious, cadaverous, per-
jured,
he was going, he was coming back, he was answering; he was
daring,
fatidic, scarlet, irresistible.

In society, in glass, in dust, in coal,
he took off; he wavered, in speaking in gold; he went up in
flames,
he rolled over, in respect;
in velvet, in weeping, he fell back.

To remember? To insist? To leave? To pardon?
Scowling he would come to
rest, rough, aghast, mural;
he was meditating to engrave himself, to become confused, to
perish.

Unattackably, with impunity,
blackly, he will sniff, he will understand;
he will orally dress;
uncertainly he will go, he will turn coward, he will forget.

¿Y bien? ¿Te sana el metaloide pálido?
¿Los metaloides incendiarios, cívicos,
inclinados al río atroz del polvo?

Esclavo, es ya la hora circular
en que las dos aurículas se forman
anillos guturales, corredizos, cuaternarios.

Señor esclavo, en la mañana mágica
se ve, por fin,
el busto de tu trémulo ronquido,
vense tus sufrimientos a caballo,
pasa el órgano bueno, el de tres asas,
hojeo, mes por mes, tu monocorde cabellera,
tu suegra llora
haciendo huesecillos de sus dedos,
se inclina tu alma con pasión a verte
y tu sien, un momento, marca el paso.

Y la gallina pone su infinito, uno por uno;
sale la tierra hermosa de las humeantes sílabas,
te retratas de pie junto a tu hermano,
truena el color oscuro bajo el lecho
y corren y entrechócanse los pulpos.

Well? The pallid metalloid heals you?
Those civic incendiary bowed
over the atrocious river of dust metalloids?

Slave, it's now the circular hour
in which your two auricles form
guttural sliding quaternary rings.

Lord slave, that magic morning
one at last sees
the bust of your tremulous snore,
your sufferings are seen on horseback,
the good organ goes by, the three-handled one,
month by month I leaf through your monochord head of hair,
your mother-in-law cries
making little bones out of her fingers,
your soul passionately leans forward to see you
and your temple, a moment, marks time.

And the hen lays her infinite, one by one;
beautiful earth comes out of the smoking syllables,
you are depicted standing next to your brother,
under the bed the dark color thunders
and the octopi race and collide.

Señor esclavo, ¿y bien?
¿Los metaloides obran en tu angustia?

27 septiembre 1937

And then, lord slave?
The metalloids work in your anguish?

¡De puro calor tengo frío,
hermana Envidia!
Lamen mi sombra leones
y el ratón me muerde el nombre,
¡madre alma mía!

¡Al borde del fondo voy,
cuñado Vicio!
La oruga tañe su voz,
y la voz tañe su oruga,
¡padre cuerpo mío!

Está de frente mi amor,
nieta Paloma!
De rodillas, mi terror
y de cabeza, mi angustia,
¡madre alma mía!

Hasta que un día sin dos,
esposa Tumba,
mi último hierro dé el son
de una víbora que duerme,
¡padre cuerpo mío . . . !

29 septiembre 1937

Of pure heat I'm freezing,
sister Envy!
Lions lick my shadow
and the mouse gnaws at my name,
my soul mother!

To the pit's edge I go,
brother-in-law Vice!
The caterpillar plays its voice
and the voice plays its caterpillar,
my flesh father!

My love is facing,
granddaughter Dove!
My terror's on its knees,
my anguish, on its head,
my soul mother!

Until a day without two,
wife Tomb,
my definitive brand hisses
like a sleeping viper,
my flesh father . . . !

Confianza en el anteojo, nó en el ojo;
en la escalera, nunca en el peldaño;
en el ala, nó en el ave
y en ti sólo, en ti sólo, en ti sólo.

Confianza en la maldad, nó en el malvado;
en el vaso, mas nunca en el licor;
en el cadáver, nó en el hombre
y en ti sólo, en ti sólo, en ti sólo.

Confianza en muchos, pero ya no en uno;
en el cauce, jamás en la corriente;
en los calzones, no en las piernas
y en ti sólo, en ti sólo, en ti sólo.

Confianza en la ventana, no en la puerta;
en la madre, mas no en los nueve meses;
en el destino, no en el dado de oro,
y en ti sólo, en ti sólo, en ti sólo.

5 octubre 1937

Confidence in glasses, nót in the eye;
in the staircase, never in the stairstep;
in the wing, nót in the bird
and in you alone, you alone, you alone.

Confidence in wickedness, nót in the wicked;
in the glass, but never in the liquor;
in the cadaver, nót in the man
and in you alone, you alone, you alone.

Confidence in many, but no longer in one;
in the bottom, never in the current;
in trousers, not in legs
and in you alone, you alone, you alone.

Confidence in the window, not in the door;
in the mother, but not in the nine months;
in destiny, not in the gold dice
and in you alone, you alone, you alone.

Terremoto

¿Hablando de la leña, callo el fuego?
¿Barriendo el suelo, olvido el fósil?
¿Razonando,
mi trenza, mi corona de carne?
(Contesta, amado Hermeregildo, el brusco;
pregunta, Luis, el lento!)

¡Encima, abajo, con tamaña altura!
¡Madera, tras el reino de las fibras!
¡Isabel, con horizonte de entrada!
¡Lejos, al lado, astutos Atanacios!

¡Todo, la parte!
Unto a ciegas en luz mis calcetines,
en riesgo, la gran paz de este peligro,
y mis cometas, en la miel pensada,
el cuerpo, en miel llorada.

¡Pregunta, Luis; responde, Hermeregildo!
¡Abajo, arriba, al lado, lejos!
¡Isabel, fuego, diplomas de los muertos!
¡Horizonte, Atanacio, parte, todo!
¡Miel de miel, llanto de frente!
¡Reino de la madera,

Earthquake

Speaking of kindling do I silence fire?
Sweeping the soil I overlook the fossil?
Reasoning,
my braid, my crown of flesh?
    (Answer, beloved Hermeregildo the Brusque;
ask, Luis the Slow!)

    Over, below, with about this height!
Wood, after the reign of the fibers!
Isabel, with entrance horizon!
Far away, to the side, astute Atanacios!

    The whole, the part!
I anoint my socks blindly in light,
in risk the great peace of this danger,
and my kites, in thought honey,
the body in wept honey.

    Ask, Luis; respond, Hermeregildo!
Below, above, to the side, far away!
Isabel, fire, diplomas of the dead!
Horizon, Atanacios, part, the whole!
Honey out of honey, cry out of forehead!
Reign of the wood

corte oblicuo a la línea del camello,
fibra de mi corona de carne!

6 octubre 1937

cut oblique to the camel line
fiber of my crown of flesh!

Escarnecido, aclimatado al bien, mórbido, hurente,
doblo el cabo carnal y juego a copas,
donde acaban en moscas los destinos,
donde comí y bebí de lo que me hunde.

Monumental adarme,
féretro numeral, los de mi deuda,
los de mi deuda, cuando caigo altamente,
ruidosamente, amoratadamente.

Al fondo, es hora,
entonces, de gemir con toda el hacha
y es entonces el año del sollozo,
el día del tobillo,
la noche del costado, el siglo del resuello.
Cualidades estériles, monótonos satanes,
del flanco brincan,
del ijar de mi yegua suplente;
¡pero, donde comí, cuánto pensé!
¡pero cuánto bebí, donde lloré!

Así es la vida, tal
como es la vida, allá, detrás
del infinito; así, espontáneamente,
delante de la sien legislativa.

Mocked, acclimatized to good, morbid, urent,
I double the carnal cable and play cups,
where the destinies end up in flies,
where I ate and drank what's cleaning me out.

Monumental dram,
numeral bier, those of my debt,
those of my debt, when I fall exceedingly,
loudly, smackedpurply.

At bottom, then,
it's time to moan with all my ax
and it's then year of the sob,
day of the ankle,
night of the rib, century of pained breath.
Sterile qualities, monotonous satans,
leap from the side,
from the flank of my sitting-in mare;
but, where I ate, how much I thought!
but, how much I drank, where I wept!

Well that's life, life
being what it is, way over there, behind
the infinite; thus, spontaneously
before the legislative temple.

Yace la cuerda así al pie del violín,
cuando hablaron del aire, a voces, cuando
hablaron muy despacio del relámpago.
Se dobla así la mala causa, vamos
de tres en tres a la unidad, así
se juega a copas
y salen a mi encuentro los que aléjanse,
acaban los destinos en bacterias
y se debe todo a todos.

7 *octubre 1937*

Thus the string lies buried at the violin's base
when they spoke of the air, shouting, when
very leisurely they spoke of lightning.
The wrong cause thus doubles, we go
three by three to unity, thus
one plays cups
and those who fold match my bet,
the destinies end up in bacteria
and one owes all to all.

Alfonso, estás mirándome, lo veo,
desde el plano implacable donde moran
lineales los siempres, lineales los jamases.
(Esa noche, dormiste, entre tu sueño
y mi sueño, en la rue de Ribouté.)
Palpablemente
tu inolvidable cholo te oye andar
en París, te siente en el teléfono callar
y toca en el alambre a tu último acto
tomar peso, brindar
por la profundidad, por mí, por ti.

Yo todavía
compro "du vin, du lait, comptant les sous"
bajo mi abrigo, para que no me vea mi alma,
bajo mi abrigo, aquel, querido Alfonso,
y bajo el rayo simple de la sien compuesta;
yo todavía sufro, y tú, ya no, jamás, hermano!
(Me han dicho que en tus siglos de dolor,
amado sér,
amado estar,
hacías ceros de madera. ¿Es cierto?)

En la "boîte de nuit," donde tocabas tangos,
tocando tu indignada criatura su corazón,
escoltado de ti mismo, llorando

Alfonso, I see you watching me
from the implacable plane where
forever and never lineally dwell.
(That night you slept between your
dream and mine on rue de Ribouté.)
Palpably
your unforgettable cholo hears you walk
in Paris, he feels you become quiet on the phone
and play on the wire your last act to
take weight, to toast
to the depths, to me, to you.

I still
buy "du vin, du lait, comptant les sous"
under my overcoat, so my soul doesn't see me,
under my overcoat, that same one, dear Alfonso,
and under the simple ray of the compound temple;
I still suffer, and you, no more, never again brother!
(They've told me in all your centuries of pain,
beloved béing,
beloved existing,
you made wood zeros. Is that true?)

In the "boîte de nuit" where you played tangos,
your provoked creature playing out its heart,
escorted by yourself, crying

por ti mismo y por tu enorme parecido con tu sombra,
monsieur Fourgat, el patrón, ha envejecido.
¿Decírselo? ¿Contárselo? No más,
Alfonso; ¡eso, ya no!

El hôtel des Ecoles funciona siempre
y todavía compran mandarinas;
pero yo sufro, como te digo,
dulcemente, recordando
lo que hubimos sufrido ambos a la muerte de ambos,
en la apertura de la doble tumba,
de esa otra tumba con tu sér,
y de ésta de caoba con tu estar;
sufro, bebiendo un vaso de ti, Silva,
un vaso para ponerse bien, como decíamos,
y después, ya veremos lo que pasa . . .

Es éste el otro brindis, entre tres,
taciturno, diverso
en vino, en mundo, en vidrio, el que brindábamos
más de una vez al cuerpo
y, menos de una vez, al pensamiento.
Hoy es más diferente todavía;
hoy sufro dulce, amargamente,
bebo tu sangre en cuanto a Cristo el duro,
como tu hueso en cuanto a Cristo el suave,
porque te quiero, dos a dos, Alfonso,
y casi lo podría decir, eternamente.

9 octubre 1937

for yourself and for your enormous resemblance to your shadow,

Monsieur Fourgat, the owner, has aged.
Tell it to him? Recount it all? Never again,
Alfonso; no more!

The hôtel des Ecoles functions as always
and they still buy mandarins;
but I suffer, like I tell you,
sweetly, remembering
what we both suffered in both our deaths,
in the aperture of the double tomb,
of that other tomb with your béing
and of this mahogany one with your existing;
I suffer drinking a glass of you, Silva,
just a glass to fix me up, as we used to say,
and afterward, then we'll see . . .

The other toast is this, between three,
taciturn, diverse
in wine, in world, in glass, the one we used to toast
more than once to the flesh
and, less than once, to the mind.
Today is even different still;
today I suffer sweet, bitterly,
I drink your blood as to Christ the hard,
I eat your bone as to Christ the soft
because I love you Alfonso, two by two,
and could almost say so eternally.

Traspie entre Dos Estrellas

¡Hay gentes tan desgraciadas, que ni siquiera
tienen cuerpo; cuantitativo el pelo,
baja, en pulgadas, la genial pesadumbre;
el modo, arriba;
no me busques, la muela del olvido,
parecen salir del aire, sumar suspiros mentalmente, oír
claros azotes en sus paladares!

Vanse de su piel, rascándose el sarcófago en que nacen
y suben por su muerte de hora en hora
y caen, a lo largo de su alfabeto gélido, hasta el suelo.

¡Ay de tanto! ¡ay de tan poco! ¡ay de ellas!
¡Ay en mi cuarto, oyéndolas con lentes!
¡Ay en mi tórax, cuando compran trajes!
¡Ay de mi mugre blanca, en su hez mancomunada!

¡Amadas sean las orejas sánchez,
amadas las personas que se sientan,
amado el desconocido y su señora,
el prójimo con mangas, cuello y ojos!

¡Amado sea aquel que tiene chinches,
el que lleva zapato roto bajo la lluvia,
el que vela el cadáver de un pan con dos cerillas,
el que se coge un dedo en una puerta,

Stumble Between Two Stars

There are people so wretched they don't even
have a body; quantitative the hair
lowers inch by inch, the genial grief;
the mode, above;
don't look for me, the molar of oblivion,
they seem to come out of the air, to add sighs mentally, to
hear
bright whips in their palates!

They leave their skin, scratching at the sarcophagus in
which they are born
and rise up through their death hour by hour
and fall, the length of their frozen alphabet, to the ground.

Aie for so much! aie for so little! aie for women!
Aie in my room hearing them with glasses on!
Aie in my thorax when they buy clothes!
Aie for my white grime, in their united scum!

Beloved be the sanchez ears,
beloved the people who sit down,
beloved the unknown man and his wife,
neighbor with sleeves, neck and eyes!

Beloved be the one who has bedbugs,
the one who wears a torn shoe in the rain,

el que no tiene cumpleaños,
el que perdió su sombra en un incendio,
el animal, el que parece un loro,
el que parece un hombre, el pobre rico,
el puro miserable, el pobre pobre!

¡Amado sea
el que tiene hambre o sed, pero no tiene
hambre con qué saciar toda su sed,
ni sed con qué saciar todas sus hambres!

¡Amado sea el que trabaja al día, al mes, a la hora,
el que suda de pena o de vergüenza,
aquel que va, por orden de sus manos, al cinema,
el que paga con lo que le falta,
el que duerme de espaldas,
el que ya no recuerda su niñez; amado sea
el calvo sin sombrero,
el justo sin espinas,
el ladrón sin rosas,
el que lleva reloj y ha visto a Dios,
el que tiene un honor y no fallece!

¡Amado sea el niño, que cae y aún llora
y el hombre que ha caído y ya no llora!

¡Ay de tanto! ¡Ay de tan poco! ¡Ay de ellos!

11 octubre 1937

the one who keeps watch over the corpse of a loaf with two matches,
the one who gets his finger caught in a door,
the one who has no birthday,
the one who lost his shadow in a fire,
the animal, the one who looks like a parrot,
the one who looks like a man, the poor rich,
the pure miserable, the poor poor!

Beloved be
the one who is hungry or thirsty, but has no
hunger with which to satiate all his thirst,
nor thirst with which to satiate all his hungers!

Beloved be the one who works by the day, by the month, by the hour,
the one who sweats from pain or from shame,
that one who goes at the command of his hands to the movies,
the one who pays with what he lacks,
the one who sleeps on his back,
the one who no longer recalls his childhood; beloved be
the bald man without a hat,
the just man without thorns,
the thief without roses,
whoever wears a wrist watch and has seen God,
who has an honor and doesn't perish!

Beloved be the child who falls and still cries
and the man who has fallen and no longer cries.

Aie for so much! Aie for so little! Aie for men!

Despedida Recordando un Adiós

Al cabo, al fin, por último,
torno, volví y acábome y os gimo, dándoos
la llave, mi sombrero, esta cartita para todos.
Al cabo de la llave está el metal en que aprendiéramos
a desdorar el oro, y está, al fin
de mi sombrero, este pobre cerebro mal peinado,
y, último vaso de humo, en su papel dramático,
yace este sueño práctico del alma.

¡Adiós, hermanos san pedros,
heráclitos, erasmos, espinozas!
¡Adiós, tristes obispos bolcheviques!
¡Adiós, gobernadores en desorden!
¡Adiós, vino que está en el agua como vino!
¡Adiós, alcohol que está en la lluvia!

¡Adiós, también, me digo a mí mismo,
adiós, vuelo formal de los milígramos!
¡También adiós, de modo idéntico,
frío del frío y frío del calor!
Al cabo, al fin, por último, la lógica,
los linderos del fuego,
la despedida recordando aquel adiós.

12 octubre 1937

Farewell Remembering a Goodbye

At the tip, in the end, terminal,
I turn, returned and finish up and moan to you, giving you
the key, my hat, this note for everyone.
At the tip of the key is the metal where we should have learned to
scratch off the gold, and there is, in the end
of my hat, this poor badly combed brain,
and, terminal glass of smoke, on its dramatic role
this practical dream of my soul rests.

Goodbye, brother san pedros,
heraclituses, erasmuses, spinozas!
Goodbye, sad bolshevik bishops!
Goodbye, disorderly governers!
Goodbye, wine that's in the water like wine!
Goodbye, alcohol that's in the rain!

Goodbye, likewise, I say to myself,
bye-bye, formal flight of milligrams!
Likewise goodbye, likewise,
cold of the cold and cold of the heat!
At the tip, in the end, terminal, the logic,
the boundaries of the fire,
the farewell remembering that goodbye.

A lo mejor, soy otro; andando, al alba, otro que marcha
en torno a un disco largo, a un disco elástico:
mortal, figurativo, audaz diafragma.
A lo mejor, recuerdo al esperar, anoto mármoles
donde índice escarlata, y donde catre de bronce,
un zorro ausente, espúreo, enojadísimo.
A lo mejor, hombre al fin,
las espaldas ungidas de añil misericordia,
a lo mejor, me digo, más allá no hay nada.

Me da la mar el disco, refiriéndolo,
con cierto margen seco, a mi garganta;
¡nada, en verdad, más ácido, más dulce, más kanteano!
Pero sudor ajeno, pero suero
o tempestad de mansedumbre,
decayendo o subiendo, eso, jamás!

Echado, fino, exhúmome,
tumefacta la mezcla en que entro a golpes,
sin piernas, sin adulto barro, ni armas,
una aguja prendida en el gran átomo . . .
¡No! ¡Nunca! ¡Nunca ayer! ¡Nunca después!

Y de ahí este tubérculo satánico,
esta muela moral de plesiosaurio

Chances are, I'm another; walking, at dawn, another who marches
around a long disk, an elastic disk:
mortal, figurative, audacious diaphragm.
Chances are, I remember when I hope, I annotate marble
where scarlet index and where bronze cot
an absent spurious infuriated fox.
Chances are, a man at last,
my shoulders anointed with merciful indigo—
chances are I'll tell myself, beyond there is nothing.

The sea hands me the disk, holding it up
with certain dry rim to my throat;
nothing, really, acrider, sweeter, more Kantian!
But another man's sweat, but a serum
or tempest of numbness,
languishing or delirious, that, never!

Laid out, slender, I exhume myself
the tumefied mixture into which I enter pounding,
without legs, without adult clay, without weapons,
a needle stuck in the great atom . . .
No! Never! Never before! Never after!

Thus this satanic tuber,
this moral plesiosaurian molar

y estas sospechas póstumas,
este índice, esta cama, estos boletos.

21 octubre 1937

and these posthumous suspicions,
this index, this bed, these tickets.

El Libro de la Naturaleza

Profesor de sollozo – he dicho a un árbol –
palo de azogue, tilo
rumoreante, a la orilla del Marne, un buen alumno
leyendo va en tu naipe, en tu hojarasca,
entre el agua evidente y el sol falso,
su tres de copas, su caballo de oros.

Rector de los capítulos del cielo,
de la mosca ardiente, de la calma manual que hay en los asnos;
rector de honda ignorancia, un mal alumno,
leyendo va en tu naipe, en tu hojarasca
el hambre de razón que le enloquece
y la sed de demencia que le aloca.

Técnico en gritos, árbol consciente, fuerte,
fluvial, doble, solar, doble, fanático,
conocedor de rosas cardinales, totalmente
metido, hasta hacer sangre, en aguijones, un alumno
leyendo va en tu naipe, en tu hojarasca,
su rey precoz, telúrico, volcánico, de espadas.

¡Oh profesor, de haber tánto ignorado!
¡Oh rector, de temblar tánto en el aire!

The Book of Nature

Professor of sob – I've said to a tree –
quicksilver stick, linden
murmuring, at the bank of the Marne, a good student
goes reading in your deck, in your dead foliage,
between the evident water and the false sun,
his three of cups, his horse of golds.

Rector of the main points of heaven,
of the ardent fly, of the manual calm there is in asses;
rector of deep ignorance, a poor student
goes reading in your deck, in your dead foliage,
the hunger for reason that maddens him
and the thirst for dementia that crazes him.

Technician in shouting, tree conscious, strong,
fluvial, double, solar, double, fanatic,
knower of cardinal roses, totally
embedded, until the blood comes, in lancings, a student
goes reading in your deck, in your dead foliage,
his precocious, telluric, volcanic king of swords.

O professor, from having overlooked só much!
O rector, from trembling só much in the air!

¡Oh técnico, de tánto que te inclinas!
¡Oh tilo! ¡Oh palo rumoroso junto al Marne!

21 octubre 1937

O technician, from só much bending over!
O linden! O murmurous stick by the Marne!

Marcha Nupcial

A la cabeza de mis propios actos,
corona en mano, batallón de dioses,
el signo negativo al cuello, atroces
el fósforo y la prisa, estupefactos
el alma y el valor, con dos impactos
al pie de la mirada; dando voces,
los límites, dinámicos, feroces;
tragándome los lloros inexactos,
me encenderé, se encenderá mi hormiga,
se encenderán mi llave, la querella
en que perdí la causa de mi huella.

Luego, haciendo del átomo una espiga,
encenderé mis hoces al pie de ella
y la espiga será por fin espiga.

22 octubre 1937

Wedding March

At the head of my own acts,
crown in hand, battalion of gods,
the negative sign on my neck, the lit
match and its haste atrocious, the soul
and the courage smacked dumb, twice thudded
at the base of her stare; screaming,
the limits dynamic, ferocious;
swallowing my inexact weeps,
I'll set myself on fire, my ant will catch,
my key, the feud in which I lost my
footprint's cause will catch. Then

shaping a wheat spike out of the atom
I'll ignite my sickles at her base
and the spike will be forever wheat.

Oye a tu masa, a tu cometa, escúchalos; no gimas
de memoria, gravísimo cetáceo;
oye a la túnica en que estás dormido,
oye a tu desnudez, dueña del sueño.

Relátate agarrándote
de la cola del fuego y a los cuernos
en que acaba la crin su atroz carrera;
rómpete, pero en círculos;
fórmate, pero en columnas combas;
descríbete atmosférico, sér de humo,
a paso redoblado de esqueleto.

¿La muerte? ¡Opónle todo tu vestido!
¿la vida? ¡Opónle parte de tu muerte!
Bestia dichosa, piensa;
dios desgraciado, quítate la frente.
Luego, hablaremos.

22 octubre 1937

Hear your mass, your kite, listen to them; don't moan
from memory, most ponderous cetacean;
hear the tunic in which you're asleep,
hear your nakedness, lady of the dream.

Report yourself holding onto the
tail of the fire and to the horns
where the mane ends its terrible race;
fracture yourself, but in circles;
form yourself, but in warped columns;
describe yourself atmospheric, béing of smoke,
in double time with your skeleton.

Death? Oppose it with all your clothes!
Life? Oppose it with part of your death!
Fortunate idiot, think;
miserable god, take off your forehead.
Then, we will talk.

Tengo un miedo terrible de ser un animal
de blanca nieve, que sostuvo padre
y madre, con su sola circulación venosa,
y que, este día espléndido, solar y arzobispal,
día que representa así a la noche,
linealmente
elude este animal estar contento, respirar
y transformarse y tener plata.

Sería pena grande
que fuera yo tan hombre hasta ese punto.
Un disparate, una premisa ubérrima
a cuyo yugo ocasional sucumbe
el gonce espiritual de mi cintura.
Un disparate . . . En tanto,
es así, más acá de la cabeza de Dios,
en la tabla de Locke, de Bacon, en el lívido pescuezo
de la bestia, en el hocico del alma.

Y, en lógica aromática,
tengo ese miedo práctico, este día
espléndido, lunar, de ser aquél, éste talvez,
a cuyo olfato huele a muerto el suelo,
el disparate vivo y el disparate muerto.

¡Oh revolcarse, estar, toser, fajarse,
fajarse la doctrina, la sien, de un hombro al otro,

I have a terrible fear of being an animal
of white snow who sustained father
and mother only with its veiny circulation,
and that this splendid solar archepiscopal day,
day that thus expresses night,
lineally
it escapes this animal to be happy, to breathe
and change itself and have money.

What a pity
if I am completely man to that point.
An absurdity, a fat premise
under whose casual yoke the spiritual
hinge of my waist succumbs.
An absurdity . . . Meanwhile
it is this way, closer than God's head
in the tabla of Locke, of Bacon, in the beast's
livid neck, in the soul's snout.

And in aromatic logic
I have this practical fear this splendid
lunar day of being that one, this one perhaps,
to whose sense of smell the soil stinks of death,
the alive absurdity and the dead absurdity.

O to thrash, to exist, to cough, to secure oneself,
secure one's doctrine, one's temple, from one shoulder to the other,

alejarse, llorar, darlo por ocho
o por siete o por seis, por cinco o darlo
por la vida que tiene tres potencias!

22 octubre 1937

to back off, to break down, to let you have it for eight
or for seven or for six, for five or give it away
for the life that holds three powers!

La cólera que quiebra al hombre en niños,
que quiebra al niño, en pájaros iguales,
y al pájaro, después, en huevecillos;
la cólera del pobre
tiene un aceite contra dos vinagres.

La cólera que al árbol quiebra en hojas,
a la hoja en botones desiguales
y al botón, en ranuras telescópicas;
la cólera del pobre
tiene dos ríos contra muchos mares.

La cólera que quiebra al bien en dudas,
a la duda, en tres arcos semejantes
y al arco, luego, en tumbas imprevistas;
la cólera del pobre
tiene un acero contra dos puñales.

La cólera que quiebra al alma en cuerpos;
al cuerpo en órganos desemejantes
y al órgano, en octavos pensamientos;
la cólera del pobre
tiene un fuego central contra dos cráteres.

27 octubre 1937

The anger that breaks man into children,
that breaks child into equal birds,
and bird, after, into little eggs;
the anger of the poor
has one oil against two vinegars.

The anger that breaks tree into leaves,
leaf into unequal buds
and bud into telescopic grooves;
the anger of the poor
has two rivers against many seas.

The anger that breaks good into doubts,
doubt into three similar arcs
and arc, then, into unforeseeable tombs;
the anger of the poor
has one steel against two daggers.

The anger that breaks soul into bodies,
body into dissimilar organs
and organ into thought eights;
the anger of the poor
has a central fire against two craters.

Intensidad y Altura

Quiero escribir, pero me sale espuma,
quiero decir muchísimo y me atollo;
no hay cifra hablada que no sea suma,
no hay pirámide escrita, sin cogollo.

Quiero escribir, pero me siento puma;
quiero laurearme, pero me encebollo.
No hay toz hablada, que no llegue a bruma,
no hay dios ni hijo de dios, sin desarrollo.

Vámonos, pues, por eso, a comer yerba,
carne de llanto, fruta de gemido,
nuestra alma melancólica en conserva.

¡Vámonos! ¡Vámonos! Estoy herido;
vámonos a beber lo ya bebido,
vámonos, cuervo, a fecundar tu cuerva.

27 octubre 1937

Intensity and Height

I want to write, but it comes out spume,
I want to say so much and I stick;
there's no cipher spoken not a sum,
no pyramid written, without neck.

I want to write, but I feel myself, puma!
I want the laurel but I'm wreathed in garlic.
There's no cough spoken that doesn't end in mist,
no god or son of god, without evolution.

Let's go then for this and feed
on grass, weep meat, groan fruit,
our melancholy soul canned.

Let's go! Let's go! I'm hit;
let's go drink that already drunk,
crow let's go fecundate your mate.

Guitarra

El placer de sufrir, de odiar, me tiñe
la garganta con plásticos venenos,
mas la cerda que implanta su orden mágico,
su grandeza taurina, entre la prima
y la sexta
y la octava mendaz, las sufre todas.

El placer de sufrir . . . ¿Quién? ¿a quién?
¿quién, las muelas? ¿a quién la sociedad,
los carburos de rabia de la encía?
¿Cómo ser
y estar, sin darle cólera al vecino?

Vales más que mi número, hombre solo,
y valen más que todo el diccionario,
con su prosa en verso,
con su verso en prosa,
tu función águila,
tu mecanismo tigre, blando prójimo.

El placer de sufrir,
de esperar esperanzas en la mesa,
el domingo con todos los idiomas,
el sábado con horas chinas, belgas,
la semana, con dos escupitajos.

Guitar

The pleasure of suffering, of hating, dyes my
throat with plastic venoms,
but the bristle that implants its magic order,
its bullfighting greatness, between the first
and the sixth
and the liar eighth, suffers them all.

The pleasure of suffering . . . Who? Whom?
who, the molars? whom, society?
the carbide of anger in the gum?
How to be
and be here, without flying into a rage at one's neighbor?

You're worth more than my number, solitary man,
and they're worth more than all the dictionary–
with its prose in verse
with its verse in prose–
your eagle function,
your tiger mechanism, bland fellowman.

The pleasure of suffering,
of hoping hopes on the table,
Sunday with all its languages,
Saturday with Chinese and Belgian hours,
the week, with two hockers.

El placer de esperar en zapatillas,
de esperar encogido tras de un verso,
de esperar con pujanza y mala saña;
el placer de sufrir: zurdazo de hembra
muerta con una piedra en la cintura
y muerta entre la cuerda y la guitarra,
llorando días y cantando meses.

28 octubre 1937

The pleasure of hoping in slippers,
of hoping hid behind a line,
of hoping with all one's thrust and blackening fury;
the pleasure of suffering: backhanded by a female
dead with a stone on her waist
and dead between string and guitar
weeping days   singing months.

¿Qué me da, que me azoto con la línea
y creo que me sigue, al trote, el punto?

¿Qué me da, que me he puesto
en los hombros un huevo en vez de un manto?

¿Qué me ha dado, que vivo?
Qué me ha dado, que muero?

¿Qué me da, que tengo ojos?
Qué me da, que tengo alma?

¿Qué me da, que se acaba en mí mi prójimo
y empieza en mi carrillo el rol del viento?

¿Qué me ha dado, que cuento mis dos lágrimas,
sollozo tierra y cuelgo el horizonte?

¿Qué me ha dado, que lloro de no poder llorar
y río de lo poco que he reído?

¿Qué me da, que ni vivo ni muero?

30 octubre 1937

What does it matter that I whip myself with the line
and believe I'm followed, at a trot, by the point?

What does it matter that I've put
an egg on my shoulder instead of a mantle?

What has it mattered that I live?
What has it mattered that I die?

What does it matter that I have eyes?
What does it matter that I have a soul?

What does it matter that my fellowman ends in me
and the list of the wind starts in my cheek?

What has it mattered that I count my two tears,
sob earth and hang the horizon?

What has it mattered that I cry from not being able to cry
and laugh at the little I've laughed?

What does it matter that I neither live nor die?

Aniversario

¡Cuánto catorce ha habido en la existencia!
¡Qué créditos con bruma en una esquina!
¡Qué diamante sintético, el del casco!
¡Cuánta más dulcedumbre
a lo largo, más honda superficie:
¡cuánto catorce ha habido en tan poco uno!

¡Qué deber,
qué cortar y qué tajo,
de memoria a memoria, en la pestaña!
¡Cuánto más amarillo, más granate!
¡Cuánto catorce en un solo catorce!

Acordeón de la tarde, en esa esquina,
piano de la mañana, aquella tarde;
clarín de carne,
tambor de un solo palo,
guitarra sin cuarta, cuánta quinta,
¡y cuánta reunión de amigos tontos
y qué nido de tigres el tabaco!
¡Cuánto catorce ha habido en la existencia!

¿Qué te diré ahora,
quince feliz, ajeno, quince de otros?
¡Nada más que no crece ya el cabello,
que han venido por las cartas,

Anniversary

How much fourteen there's been in existence!
What we believed in the fog on a corner!
What a synthetic diamond the skull is!
How much more sweetness
lengthwise, deeper surface:
how much fourteen there's been in so little one!

What to owe,
what to divide and what a notch
from memory to memory, in one's eyelash!
How much more yellow, more garnet!
How much fourteen in a single fourteen!

Accordion of the evening, on that corner,
piano of the morning, more distant evening;
bugle of flesh,
drum of a single stick,
penniless guitar, what villas,
how much reunion fooling with friends,
what a nest of tigers that tobacco was!
How much fourteen there's been in existence!

What to say to you now,
happy fifteen, alien, fifteen of others?
Just that my hair no longer grows,
that they've come for the letters,

que me brillan los seres que he parido,
que no hay nadie en mi tumba
y que me han confundido con mi llanto!

¡Cuánto catorce ha habido en la existencia!

31 octubre 1937

that the beings I've brought forth shine at me,
that there's no one in my tomb
and that they've confused *me* with my weeping!

How much fourteen there's been in existence!

Panteón

He visto ayer sonidos generales,
mortuoriamente,
puntualmente alejarse,
cuando oí desprenderse del ocaso
tristemente,
exactamente un arco, un arcoíris.

Ví el tiempo generoso del minuto,
infinitamente
atado locamente al tiempo grande
pues que estaba la hora
suavemente,
premiosamente henchida de dos horas.

Dejóse comprender, llamar, la tierra
terrenalmente;
negóse brutalmente así a mi historia,
y si ví, que me escuchen, pues, en bloque,
si toque esta mecánica, que vean
lentamente,
despacio, vorazmente, mis tinieblas.

Y si ví en la lesión de la respuesta,
claramente,
la lesión mentalmente de la incógnita,
si escuché, si pensé en mis ventanillas

Pantheon

I've seen yesterday general sounds
mortuarily,
punctually recede,
when I heard rip loose from the sunsetting
sadly,
exactly a rain, a rainbów.

I saw the minute's generous time
infinitely
tied insanely to great time
for the hour was
gently,
urgently swollen with two hours.

The earth allowed herself to be comprehended,
named, terrainly;
she denied, thus, brutally, my history,
and if I saw, let them hear me then in block,
if I touched this mechanics, let them see
slowly,
slow, voraciously, my darknesses.

And if I saw in the lesion of the response
clearly,
the lesion, mentally, of the unknown,
if I heard, if I thought, in my nasal

nasales, funerales, temporales,
fraternalmente,
piadosamente echadme a los filósofos.

Mas no más inflexión precipitada
en canto llano, y no más
el hueso colorado, el son del alma
tristemente
erguida ecuestremente en mi espinazo,
ya que, en suma, la vida es
implacablemente,
imparcialmente horrible, estoy seguro.

31 octubre 1937

funereal, temporal, peepholes,
fraternally,
piously, toss me to the philosophers.

But no more precipitate inflection
in plain song, and no more
red bone, the sound of the soul
sadly
straightened equestrianly in my spine,
now that, in sum, life is
implacably,
impartially hideous, I'm sure.

Dos Niños Anhelantes

No. No tienen tamaño sus tobillos; no es su espuela
suavísima, que da en las dos mejillas.
Es la vida no más, de bata y yugo.

No. No tiene plural su carcajada,
ni por haber salido de un molusco perpétuo, aglutinante,
ni por haber entrado al mar descalza,
es la que piensa y marcha, es la finita.
Es la vida no más; sólo la vida.

Lo sé, lo intuyo cartesiano, autómata,
moribundo, cordial, en fin, espléndido.
Nada hay
sobre la ceja cruel de su esqueleto;
nada, entre lo que dió y tomó con guante
la paloma, y con guante,
la eminente lombriz aristotélica;
nada delante ni detrás del yugo;
nada de mar en el océano
y nada
en el orgullo grave de la célula.
Sólo la vida; así: cosa bravísima.

Plenitud inextensa,
alcance abstracto, venturoso, de hecho,
glacial y arrebatado, de la llama;

Two Anxious Children

No. Its ankles have no size; it's not its softest
spur that digs in both cheeks.
It's just life, from dressing gown and yoke.

No. Its guffaw has no plural,
not for having come out of a perpetual agglutinating mollusk,
nor for having entered the sea barefoot,
it's that that thinks and goes on, it's the finite.
It's just life; only life.

I know it, intuit it Cartesian, automaton,
about to die, cordial, in short, magnificent.
Nothing is
over the cruel brow of its skeleton;
nothing between what the dove gave
and took back with a glove on, and with a glove too
the eminent Aristotelian earthworm;
nothing in front of or behind the yoke;
nothing of the sea in the ocean
and nothing
in the grave pride of the cell.
Only life; thus: a terrible struggle.

Abundance limited,
range abstract, fortunate, in fact
glacial and impetuous, from the flame;

freno del fondo, rabo de la forma.
Pero aquello
para lo cual nací ventilándome
y crecí con afecto y drama propios,
mi trabajo rehúsalo,
mi sensación y mi arma lo involucran.
Es la vida y no más, fundada, escénica.

Y por este rumbo,
su serie de órganos extingue mi alma
y por este indecible, endemoniado cielo,
mi maquinaria da silbidos técnicos,
paso la tarde en la mañana triste
y me esfuerzo, palpito, tengo frío.

2 noviembre 1937

brake of the depths, tail of form.
But that
for which I was born ventilating myself
and grew with my own tenderness and drama,
my work rejects,
my feelings and my weapon involucrate.
It is life and that's all, established, scenic.

And through this direction
its series of organs extinguish my soul
and through this inexpressible demonized sky
my machinery emits technical hisses.
I spend my evening in the sad morning
and I struggle, I shudder, I'm cold.

Un hombre está mirando a una mujer,
está mirándola inmediatamente,
con su mal de tierra suntuosa
y la mira a dos manos
y la tumba a dos pechos
y la mueve a dos hombros.

Pregúntome entonces, oprimiéndome
la enorme, blanca, acérrima costilla:
Y este hombre
¿no tuvo a un niño por creciente padre?
¿Y esta mujer, a un niño
por constructor de su evidente sexo?

Puesto que un niño veo ahora,
niño ciempiés, apasionado, enérgico:
veo que no le ven
sonarse entre los dos, colear, vestirse;
puesto que los acepto,
a ella en condición aumentativa,
a él en la flexión del heno rubio.

Y exclamo entonces, sin cesar ni uno
de vivir, sin volver ni uno
a temblar en la justa que venero:
¡Felicidad seguida

A man is watching a woman,
is watching her immediately
with his sumptuous land sickness
and he watches her two-handedly
and he knocks her over two-breastedly
and he moves her two-shoulderedly.

I ask myself then, pressing down
my enormous, white, steel rib:
And hadn't this man
a child as a growing father?
And this woman, a child
as builder of her evident sex?

For I now see a child,
energetic, impassioned, centipede child:
I see they fail to see it
sound itself between them, wriggle, dress itself;
for I accept them,
her in augmentative condition,
him in the flexion of the blond hay.

And I cry out then, without stopping even one
from living, without turning even one
to tremble in the joust I venerate:
Happiness followed

tardíamente del Padre,
del Hijo y de la Madre!
¡Instante redondo,
familiar, que ya nadie siente ni ama!
¡De qué deslumbramiento áfono, tinto,
se ejecuta el cantar de los cantares!
¡De qué tronco, el florido carpintero!
¡De qué perfecta axila, el frágil remo!
¡De qué casco, ambos cascos delanteros!

2 noviembre 1937

belatedly by the Father,
by the Son and by the Mother!
Round instant,
familiar, that now no one feels or loves!
From what silent, dyed clear light
rings out the Song of Songs!
From what a trunk, the florid carpenter!
From what a perfect axilla, the fragile oar!
From what a skull, both skull forwarders!

Los Nueve Monstruos

Y, desgraciadamente,
el dolor crece en el mundo a cada rato,
crece a treinta minutos por segundo, paso a paso,
y la naturaleza del dolor, es el dolor dos veces
y la condición del martirio, carnívoro, voraz,
es el dolor, dos veces
y la función de la yerba purísima, el dolor
dos veces
y el bien de sér, dolernos doblemente.

¡Jamás, hombres humanos,
hubo tánto dolor en el pecho, en la solapa, en la cartera,
en el vaso, en la carnicería, en la aritmética!
¡Jamás tánto cariño doloroso,
jamás tan cerca arremetió lo lejos,
jamás el fuego nunca
jugó mejor su rol de frío muerto!
¡Jamás, señor ministro de salud, fué la salud
más mortal
y la migraña extrajo tánta frente de la frente!
Y el mueble tuvo en su cajón, dolor,
el corazón, en su cajón, dolor,
la lagartija, en su cajón, dolor.

¡Crece la desdicha, hermanos hombres,
más pronto que la máquina, a diez máquinas, y crece

The Nine Monsters

And, unfortunately,
pain grows in the world every moment,
grows thirty minutes a second, step by step,
and the nature of the pain is the pain twice
and the condition of the voracious carnivorous martyrdom
the pain, twice
and the function of the very pure grass, the pain
twice
and the good of béing, to bend us double.

Never, human men,
was there so múch pain in the chest, in the lapel, in the wallet,
in the glass, in the butcher's, in arithmetic!
Never so múch painful tenderness,
never did what is far rush so close,
never did the fire ever
play better its role of dead cold!
Never, mister minister of health, was health
more mortal,
did the migraine extract so múch forehead from the forehead!
did furniture have in its drawer, pain,
the heart in its drawer, pain,
the newt in its drawer, pain.

The wretchedness grows, man brothers,
sooner than the machine, than ten machines, and it grows

con la res de Rousseau, con nuestras barbas;
crece el mal por razones que ignoramos
y es una inundación con propios líquidos,
con propio barro y propia nube sólida!
Invierte el sufrimiento posiciones, da función
en que el humor acuoso es vertical
al pavimiento,
el ojo es visto y esta oreja oída,
y esta oreja da nueve campanadas a la hora
del rayo, y nueve carcajadas
a la hora del trigo, y nueve sones hembras
a la hora del llanto, y nueve cánticos
a la hora del hambre, y nueve truenos
y nueve látigos, menos un grito.

El dolor nos agarra, hermanos hombres,
por detrás, de perfil,
y nos aloca en los cinemas,
nos clava en los gramófonos,
nos desclava en los lechos, cae perpendicularmente
a nuestros boletos, a nuestras cartas;
y es muy grave sufrir, puede uno orar . . .
Pues de resultas
del dolor, hay algunos
que nacen, otros crecen, otros mueren,
y otros que nacen y no mueren y otros
que sin haber nacido, mueren, y otros
que no nacen ni mueren (Son los más).
¡Y también de resultas
del sufrimiento, estoy triste
hasta la cabeza, y más triste hasta el tobillo,
de ver al pan, crucificado, al nabo,
ensangrentado,
llorando, a la cebolla,
al cereal, en general, harina,
a la sal, hecha polvo, al agua, huyendo,

with the cattle-head of Rousseau, with our beards;
evil grows for reasons we know not
and is a flood with its own liquids,
its own clay, its own solid cloud!
Suffering inverts positions, stages shows
in which the watery humour is vertical
to the pavement,
the eye is seen and this ear heard,
and this ear strikes nine times at the hour
of lightning, nine funhouse roars
at the hour of wheat, nine female sounds
at the hour of weeping, nine canticles
at the hour of hunger, nine thunders
nine whips, minus a cry.

The pain grabs us, man brothers,
from behind, in profile,
and drives us crazy in the movies,
nails us up on the gramophones,
pries us loose in bed, falls perpendicularly
to our tickets, to our letters;
and it is very serious to suffer, one can pray . . .
So because
of the pain there are some
who get born, others grow, others die,
and others that get born and don't die and others
who without having been born die and others
who neither get born nor die (The majority).
And likewise because
of the suffering I'm sad
to my head and sadder to my ankle
seeing bread crucified, the turnip
bloodsmeared,
weeping, the onion,
cereal, in general, flour,
salt turned dust, water fleeing,

al vino, un ecce-homo,
tan pálida a la nieve, al sol tan ardio!
¡Cómo, hermanos humanos,
no deciros que ya no puedo y
ya no puedo con tánto cajón,
tánto minuto, tánta
lagartija y tánta
inversión, tánto lejos y tánta sed de sed!
Señor Ministro de Salud: ¿qué hacer?
¡Ah! desgraciadamente, hombre humanos,
hay, hermanos, muchísimo que hacer.

3 noviembre 1937

wine an Ecce-homo,
the snow so pallid, such a red red sun!
How, human brothers,
not to tell you that I can't stand anymore and
I can't stand anymore with so múch drawer,
So múch minute, so múch
newt and so
múch inversion, so múch far, so múch thirst for more thirst!
Mister Minister of Health: what to do?
Ah! unfortunately, human men,
brothers, there is much too much to do.

Un hombre pasa con un pan al hombro.
¿Voy a escribir, después, sobre mi doble?

Otro se sienta, ráscase, extrae un piojo de su axila, mátalo.
¿Con qué valor hablar del psicoanálisis?

Otro ha entrado a mi pecho con un palo en la mano.
¿Hablar luego de Sócrates al médico?

Un cojo pasa dando el brazo a un niño.
¿Voy, después, a leer a André Breton?

Otro tiembla de frío, tose, escupe sangre.
¿Cabrá aludir jamás al Yo profundo?

Otro busca en el fango huesos, cáscaras.
¿Cómo escribir, después, del infinito?

Un albañil cae de un techo, muere y ya no almuerza.
¿Innovar, luego, el tropo, la metáfora?

Un comerciante roba un gramo en el peso a un cliente.
¿Hablar, después, de cuarta dimensión?

Un banquero falsea su balance.
¿Con qué cara llorar en el teatro?

A man walks by with a loaf of bread on his shoulder.
I'm going to write, after that, about my double?

Another sits, scratches, gets a louse out of his armpit,
cracks it. How dare one speak about psychoanalysis?

Another has entered my chest with a stick in his hand.
After that chat with the doctor about Socrates?

A cripple walks by arm in arm with a child.
After that I'm going to read André Breton?

Another shakes from cold, hacks, spits blood.
Is it possible to even mention the profound I?

Another searches in the mud for bones, rinds.
How write after that about the infinite?

A bricklayer falls from the roof, dies, and no longer eats
lunch.
After that innovate the trope, the metaphor?

A merchant cheats a customer out of a gram.
After that talk about the fourth dimension?

A banker falsifies his balance.
With what face to cry in the theater?

Un paria duerme con el pie a la espalda.
¿Hablar, después, a nadie de Picasso?

Alguien va en un entierro sollozando.
¿Cómo luego ingresar a la Academia?

Alguien limpia un fusil en su cocina.
¿Con qué valor hablar del más allá?

Alguien pasa contando con sus dedos.
¿Cómo hablar del no-yó sin dar un grito?

5 noviembre 1937

An outcast sleeps with his foot behind his back.
After that, not talk about Picasso?

Someone goes to a burial sobbing.
How then enter the Academy?

Someone cleans a rifle in his kitchen.
How dare one speak about the beyond?

Someone walks by counting on his fingers.
How speak of the not-I without crying out?

Me viene, hay días, una gana ubérrima, política,
de querer, de besar al cariño en sus dos rostros,
y me viene de lejos un querer
demostrativo, otro querer amar, de grado o fuerza,
al que me odia, al que rasga su papel, al muchachito,
a la que llora por el que lloraba,
al rey del vino, al esclavo del agua,
al que ocultóse en su ira,
al que suda, al que pasa, al que sacude su persona en mi alma.
Y quiero, por lo tanto, acomodarle
al que me habla, su trenza; sus cabellos, al soldado;
su luz, al grande; su grandeza, al chico.
Quiero planchar directamente
un pañuelo al que no puede llorar
y, cuando estoy triste o me duele la dicha,
remendar a los niños y a los genios.

Quiero ayudar al bueno a ser su poquillo de malo
y me urge estar sentado
a la diestra del zurdo, y responder al mudo,
tratando de serle útil en
lo que puedo, y también quiero muchísimo
lavarle al cojo el pie,
y ayudarle a dormir al tuerto próximo.

There comes over me days a feeling so abundant, political,
for passion, for kissing tenderness on its two faces,
and comes over me from far away a demonstrative
passion, other passion to love, willingly or by force,
whoever hates me, whoever tears up the child's paper,
the woman who weeps for the man who was weeping,
the wine king, the water slave,
whoever hid in his wrath,
whoever sweats, whoever walks by, whoever shakes himself
in my soul.
And I want, of course, to settle
the braid for whoever talks to me; the soldier's hair;
the light of the great; the greatness of the kid.
I want to iron right off
a handkerchief for whoever can't weep
and when I'm sad or happiness hurts me
to mend the children and the geniuses.

I want to help the good man be his little bad
and I need to be seated to
the right of the lefthanded and respond to the dumb,
trying to be useful to that man in
some way, and also I want very
much to wash the cripple's foot
and help my one-eyed neighbor sleep.

¡Ah querer, éste, el mío, éste, el mundial,
interhumano y parroquial, proyecto!
Me viene al pelo,
desde el cimiento, desde la ingle pública,
y, viniendo de lejos, da ganas de besarle
la bufanda al cantor,
y al que sufre, besarle en su sartén,
al sordo, en su rumor craneano, impávido;
al que me da lo que olvidé en mi seno,
en su Dante, en su Chaplin, en sus hombros.

Quiero, para terminar,
cuando estoy al borde célebre de la violencia
o lleno de pecho el corazón, querría
ayudar a reír al que sonríe,
ponerle un pajarillo al malvado en plena nuca,
cuidar a los enfermos enfadándolos,
comprarle al vendedor,
ayudarle a matar al matador – cosa terrible –
y quisiera yo ser bueno conmigo
en todo.

6 noviembre 1937

Ah to love this man, mine, this man, the
ancient interhuman parochial world's!
Wells up to my hair
from the foundation, from the public groin,
and coming from far away makes me feel like kissing
the singer's muffler,
whoever suffers, to kiss him in his frying pan,
the deaf man in his courageous cranial murmur;
whoever gives me what I forgot in my breast
in his Dante, in his Chaplin, in his shoulders.

I want, in order to end,
when I'm at violence's celebrated edge
or my heart swollen size of my chest, I'd like
to help laugh whoever smiles,
to put a little bird smack on the bastard's neck,
to care for the sick exasperating them,
to buy from the salesman,
to help the killer kill – terrible thing –
and to have been in everything
straight with myself.

Hoy le ha entrado una astilla.
Hoy le ha entrado una astilla cerca, dándole
cerca, fuerte, en su modo
de ser y en su centavo ya famoso.
Le ha dolido la suerte mucho,
todo;
le ha dolido la puerta,
le ha dolido la faja, dándole
sed, aflicción
y sed del vaso pero no del vino.
Hoy le salió a la pobre vecina del aire,
a escondidas, humareda de su dogma;
hoy le ha entrado una astilla.

La inmensidad persíguela
a distancia superficial, a un vasto eslabonazo.
Hoy le salió a la pobre vecina del viento,
en la mejilla, norte, y en la mejilla, oriente;
hoy le ha entrado una astilla.

¿Quien comprará, en los días perecederos, ásperos,
un pedacito de café con leche,
y quién, sin ella, bajará a su rastro hasta dar luz?
¿Quién será, luego, sábado, a las siete?
¡Tristes son las astillas que le entran
a uno,

Today a splinter has entered her.
Today a splinter has entered her near, hitting her
near, hard, in her way
of béing and in her now famed centavo.
Fate's hurt her much,
everything;
the door's hurt her,
her binding's hurt her, giving her
thirst, affliction
and thirst for the glass but not for the wine.
Today the poor neighbor of the air's dogma
secretly started to billow smoke;
today a splinter has entered her.

The immensity pursues her
at a superficial distance, at a vast link-blow.
Today north appeared on the poor
neighbor of the wind's cheek
and on her cheek, orient;
today a splinter has entered her.

Who'll buy, in these raw fleeting days,
a little piece of coffee with cream,
and who, without her, will go down his trace until he lights?
Who will it be, then, Saturday, at seven?
Sad are the splinters that enter
one,

exactamente ahí precisamente!
Hoy le entró a la pobre vecina de viaje,
una llama apagada en el oráculo;
hoy le ha entrado una astilla.

Le ha dolido el dolor, el dolor joven,
el dolor niño, el dolorazo, dándole
en las manos
y dándole sed, aflicción
y sed del vaso, pero no del vino.
¡La pobre pobrecita!

6 noviembre 1937

exactly there precisely!
Today a flame quenched in the oracle
entered the poor neighbor of the voyage;
today a splinter has entered her.

The hurt has hurt her, the young hurt,
the child hurt, the dead hurt, hitting her
in her hands
and giving her thirst, affliction
and thirst for the glass, but not for the wine.
Christ, that poor woman!

El Alma que Sufrió de Ser su Cuerpo

Tu sufres de una glándula endocrínica, se ve,
o, quizá,
sufres de mí, de mi sagacidad escueta, tácita.
Tú padeces del diáfano antropoide, allá, cerca,
donde está la tiniebla tenebrosa.
Tú das vuelta al sol, agarrándote el alma,
extendiendo tus juanes corporales
y ajustándote el cuello; eso se ve.
Tú sabes lo que te duele,
lo que te salta al anca,
lo que baja por ti con soga al suelo.
Tú, pobre hombre, vives; no lo niegues,
si mueres; ¡no lo niegues,
si mueres de tu edad! ¡ay! y de tu época.
Y, aunque llores, bebes,
y, aunque sangres, alimentas a tu híbrido colmillo,
a tu vela tristona y a tus partes.
Tú sufres, tú padeces y tú vuelves a sufrir horriblemente,
desgraciado mono,
jovencito de Darwin,
alguacil que me atisbas, atrocísimo microbio.
Y tú lo sabes a tal punto,
que lo ignoras, soltándote a llorar.
Tú, luego, has nacido; eso
también se ve de lejos, infeliz y cállate,
y soportas la calle que te dió la suerte
a tu ombligo interrogas: ¿dónde? ¿cómo?

The Soul That Suffered from Being Its Body

You suffer from an endocrine gland, that's obvious,
or, perhaps,
suffer from me, from my tacit tight-lipped sagacity.
You suffer from the transparent anthropoid, there, near,
where is tenebrous darkness.
You walk around the sun, grabbing onto your soul,
holding out your corporeal juanes
and tightening your collar; that's obvious.
You know what hurts you,
what leaps and mounts you,
what lowers through you with a rope to the ground.
You, poor man, you live; don't deny it,
if you die; don't deny it,
if you die from your age, ay! and from your times.
And even if you cry, you drink,
even if you bleed you feed your hybrid fang,
your big sad candle and your parts.
You suffer, you endure, and again you suffer horribly,
poor unhappy ape,
Darwin's little Fauntleroy,
sheriff with an eye on me, most disgusting microbe.
And you know this so well
you ignore it, releasing into tears.
You, then, have been born; that
too is too obvious, luckless and shut up
and stand the street fate gave you,
you question your navel: where? how?

Amigo mío, estás completamente,
hasta el pelo, en el año treinta y ocho,
nicolás o santiago, tal o cual,
estés contigo o con tu aborto o conmigo
y cautivo en tu enorme libertad,
arrastrado por tu hércules autónomo . . .
Pero si tú calculas en tus dedos hasta dos,
es peor; no lo niegues, hermanito.

¿Que nó? ¿Que sí, pero que nó?
¡Pobre mono! . . . ¡Dame la pata! . . . No. La mano, he dicho.
¡Salud! ¡Y sufre!

8 noviembre 1937

My friend, you're completely up
to your hair in the 38th year,
nicolas or santiago, such or which,
whether you're with yourself or with your abortion or with me,
and caught in your enormous freedom,
dragged on by your autonomous hercules . . .
But if you calculate on your fingers up to two,
it's worse; don't deny it, little brother.

Nó? Yes but nó?
Poor ape! . . . Gimme your paw! . . . No. The hand, I said.
Cheers! And suffer!

Palmas y Guitarras

Ahora, entre nosotros, aquí,
ven conmigo, trae por la mano a tu cuerpo
y cenemos juntos y pasemos un instante la vida
a dos vidas y dando una parte a nuestra muerte.
Ahora, ven contigo, hazme el favor
de quejarte en mi nombre y a la luz de la noche tenebrosa
en que traes a tu alma de la mano
y huímos en puntillas de nosotros.

Ven a mí, sí, y a ti, sí,
con paso par, a vernos a los dos con paso impar,
marcar el paso de la despedida.
¡Hasta cuando volvamos! ¡Hasta la vuelta!
¡Hasta cuando leamos, ignorantes!
¡Hasta cuando volvamos, despidámonos!

¿Qué me importan los fusiles,
escúchame;
escúchame, qué impórtanme,
si la bala circula ya en el rango de mi firma?
¿Qué te importan a ti las balas,
si el fusil está humeando ya en tu olor?
Hoy mismo pesaremos
en los brazos de un ciego nuestra estrella
y, una vez que me cantes, lloraremos.
Hoy mismo, hermosa, con tu paso par

Palms and Guitars

Now, between us, here,
come with me, bring your body by the hand
and let's eat together and pass life a moment
to two lives, giving a portion to our death.
Now, come with me, please
complain in my name and by the light of the tenebrous night
in which you bring your soul with your hand
and we flee on tiptoes from ourselves.

Come to me, yes, and to you, yes,
in step, to see the two of us out of step,
to mark time of the goodbye.
Until we return! Until the turn!
Until we read, ignorant!
Until we return, let's say goodbye!

What are the rifles to me,
listen to me;
listen to me, what's it to me
if the bullet's now circling in my signature's rank?
What are the bullets to you
if the rifle's smoking now in your odor?
This very day we'll weigh in
the arms of a blind man our star
and the one time you sing to me, we'll cry.
This very day, beautiful, with your in-step

y tu confianza a que llegó mi alarma,
saldremos de nosotros, dos a dos.
¡Hasta cuando seamos ciegos!
¡Hasta
que lloremos de tánto volver!

Ahora,
entre nosotros, trae
por la mano a tu dulce personaje
y cenemos juntos y pasemos un instante la vida
a dos vidas y dando una parte a nuestra muerte.
Ahora, ven contigo, hazme el favor
de cantar algo
y de tocar en tu alma, haciendo palmas.
¡Hasta cuando volvamos! ¡Hasta entonces!
¡Hasta cuando partamos, despidámonos!

8 noviembre 1937

and your trust reached by my alarm,
we'll come out of ourselves, two by two.
Until we become blind men!
Until
we cry from turning turning!

Now,
between us, bring
your sweet way by the hand
and let's eat together and pass life a moment
to two lives, giving a portion to our death.
Now, come with yourself, please
sing something
and strum your soul, snapping palms.
Until we return! Until then!
Until we part, let's say goodbye!

Yuntas

Completamente. Además, ¡vida!
Completamente. Además, ¡muerte!

Completamente. Además, ¡todo!
Completamente. Además, ¡nada!

Completamente. Además, ¡mundo!
Completamente. Además, ¡polvo!

Completamente. Además, ¡Dios!
Completamente. Además, ¡nadie!

Completamente. Además, ¡nunca!
Completamente. Además, ¡siempre!

Completamente. Además, ¡oro!
Completamente. Además, ¡humo!

Completamente. Además, ¡lágrimas!
Completamente. Además, ¡risas! . . .

Completamente!

9 noviembre 1937

Yokes

Completely. Furthermore, life!
Completely. Furthermore, death!

Completely. Furthermore, everything!
Completely. Furthermore, nothing!

Completely. Furthermore, world!
Completely. Furthermore, dust!

Completely. Furthermore, God!
Completely. Furthermore, no one!

Completely. Furthermore, never!
Completely. Furthermore, always!

Completely. Furthermore, gold!
Completely. Furthermore, smoke!

Completely. Furthermore, tears!
Completely. Furthermore, laughs! . . .

Completely!

Acaba de pasar el que vendrá
proscrito, a sentarse en mi triple desarrollo;
acaba de pasar criminalmente.

Acaba de sentarse más acá,
a un cuerpo de distancia de mi alma,
el que vino en un asno a enflaquecerme;
acaba de sentarse de pie, lívido.

Acaba de darme lo que está acabado,
el calor del fuego y el pronombre inmenso
que el animal crió bajo su cola.

Acaba
de expresarme su duda sobre hipótesis lejanas
que él aleja, aún más, con la mirada.

Acaba de hacer al bien los honores que le tocan
en virtud del infame paquidermo,
por lo soñado en mí y en él matado.

Acaba de ponerme (no hay primera)
su segunda aflixxión en plenos lomos
y su tercer sudor en plena lágrima.

The one who will come just passed
banished, to sit down on my triple unwinding;
he just passed criminally.

He just sat down nearer,
a body away from my soul,
the one who came on a donkey to drain me
just sat down on foot, livid.

He just gave me what is over,
the heat of the fire and the immense pronoun
the animal nurtured under its tail.

He just
expressed his doubts to me concerning remote hypotheses
that he withdraws, even more, with his look.

He just bestowed on the good its rightful honors
by virtue of the foul pachyderm
through what is dreamed in me and in him murdered.

He just fixed (there is no first)
his second afflixxion right in my shoulders
and his third sweat right in my tear.

Acaba de pasar sin haber venido.

12 noviembre 1937

He just passed without having come.

¡Ande desnudo, en pelo, el millonario!
¡Desgracia al que edifica con tesoros su lecho de muerte!
¡Un mundo al que saluda;
un sillón al que siembra en el cielo;
llanto al que da término a lo que hace, guardando los comienzos;
ande el de las espuelas;
poco dure muralla en que no crezca otra muralla;
dése al mísero toda su miseria,
pan, al que ríe;
hayan perder los triunfos y morir los médicos;
haya leche en la sangre;
añádase una vela al sol,
ochocientos al veinte;
pase la eternidad bajo los puentes!
¡Desdén al que viste,
corónense los pies de manos, quepan en su tamaño;
siéntese mi persona junto a mí!
¡Llorar al haber cabido en aquel vientre,
bendición al que mira aire en el aire,
muchos años de clavo al martillazo;
desnúdese el desnudo,
vístase de pantalón la capa,
fulja el cobre a expensas de sus láminas,
majestad al que cae de la arcilla al universo,
lloren las bocas, giman las miradas,

Let the millionaire walk naked, barebacked!
Disgrace to the one who builds his deathbed with treasures!
A world to the one who greets;
an armchair to the one who sows in the sky;
tears for the one who finishes what he does, keeping the beginnings;
spur-wearer walk!
won't last long wall on which another wall isn't growing;
give to the miserable all his misery,
bread to the one who laughs;
make the triumphs lose and the doctors die;
milk be in blood;
add a candle to the sun,
eight hundred to the twenty;
eternity pass under the bridges!
Scorn to the one who wears clothes,
crown the feet with hands, fit them in their size;
myself sit next to me!
To weep having fit in that belly,
blessings for the one who sees air in air,
many years of nail to the hammer-stroke;
strip the naked,
dress the cape in pants,
shine the copper at expense of its leaf,
royalty to the one who falls from clay to universe,
mouths weep, looks groan,

impídase al acero perdurar,
hilo a los horizontes portátiles,
doce ciudades al sendero de piedra,
una esfera al que juega con su sombra;
un día hecho de una hora, a los esposos;
una madre al arado en loor al suelo,
séllense con dos sellos a los líquidos,
pase lista el bocado,
sean los descendientes,
sea la codorniz,
sea la carrera del álamo y del árbol;
venzan, al contrario del círculo, el mar a su hijo
y a la cana el lloro;
dejad los áspides, señores hombres,
surcad la llama con los siete leños,
vivid,
elévese la altura,
baje el hondor más hondo,
conduzca la onda su impulsión andando,
tenga éxito la tregua de la bóveda!
¡Muramos;
lavad vuestro esqueleto cada día;
no me hagáis caso,
una ave coja al déspota y a su alma;
una mancha espantosa, al que va solo;
gorriones al astrónomo, al gorrión, al aviador!
¡Lloved, solead,
vigilad a Júpiter, al ladrón de ídolos de oro,
copiad vuestra letra en tres cuadernos,
aprended de los cónyuges cuando hablan, y
de los solitarios, cuando callan;
dad de comer a los novios,
dad de beber al diablo en vuestras manos,
luchad por la justicia con la nuca,
igualaos,
cúmplase el roble,

stop that steel from enduring,
thread to the portable horizons,
twelve cities to the stone path,
a sphere for the one who plays with his shadow;
a one-hour day for the husband and wife;
a mother for the plow in praise of soil,
seal the liquids with two seals,
let the mouthful inspect,
the descendants be,
the quail be,
the race of the poplar be, the tree be;
counter to the circle the sea conquer its son
and weeping the grey hair;
release the asps, mister men,
harrow your blaze with the seven logs,
live,
the height raise,
the depth lower deeper,
the wave drive its impulsion walking,
the vault's truce succeed!
Let's die;
scrub your skeleton each day;
pay no attention to me,
a bird grab the despot and his soul;
a terrifying stain to the one who goes alone;
sparrows to the astronomer, to the sparrow, to the aviator!
Let rain rain, sun sun!
keep an eye on Jupiter, on the thief of your gold idols,
copy your letter in three notebooks,
learn from the married folks when they speak, and
from the lonely, when they're quiet;
give the sweethearts something to eat,
give the devil in your hands something to drink,
fight for justice with your nape,
equalize yourselves,
let the oak be done,

cúmplase el leopardo entre dos robles,
seamos,
estémos,
sentid cómo navega el agua en los océanos,
alimentaos,
concíbase el error, puesto que lloro,
acéptese, en tanto suban por el risco, las cabras y sus crías;
desacostumbrad a Dios a ser un hombre,
creced . . . !
Me llaman. Vuelvo.

19 noviembre 1937

let the leopard between two oaks be done,
let us be,
let us be here,
feel how the water sails in the oceans,
nourish yourselves,
conceive the error, since I'm weeping,
accept it while goats and kids still clamber about the cliffs;
make God break the habit of being a man,
grow up . . . !
They're calling me. I'll be back.

Viniere el malo, con un trono al hombro,
y el bueno, a acompañar al malo a andar;
dijeren "sí" el sermón, "no" la plegaria
y cortare el camino en dos la roca . . .

Comenzare por monte la montaña,
por remo el tallo, por timón el cedro
y esperaren doscientos a sesenta
y volviere la carne a sus tres títulos . . .

Sobrase nieve en la noción del fuego,
se acostare el cadáver a mirarnos,
la centella a ser trueno corpulento
y se arquearen los saurios a ser aves . . .

Faltare excavación junto al estiércol,
naufragio al río para resbalar,
cárcel al hombre libre, para serlo
y una atmósfera al cielo, y hierro al oro . . .

Mostraren disciplina, olor, las fieras,
se pintare el enojo de soldado,
me dolieren el junco que aprendí,
la mentira que inféctame y socórreme . . .

If the evil one came with a throne on his shoulder
and the good one, to accompany the evil one in going;
if they affirmed the sermon and denied the prayer
and the road cut the rock in two . . .

If the mountain began as a hill,
as oar the stem, as tiller the cedar,
if two hundred waited for sixty
and the flesh returned to its three titles . . .

If there was too much snow in the notion of fire,
if the cadaver lay down to watch us,
if the flash was corpulent thunder
and the saurians arched to be birds . . .

If excavation were lacking next to dung,
shipwreck to the river so to slip,
jail to the free man, so to be free,
an atmosphere to the sky, iron to gold . . .

If wild beasts showed odor and discipline,
if the soldier's anger could be painted,
if the reed I learned ached me,
the lie that infects me and corrodes me . . .

Sucediere ello así y así poniéndolo,
¿con qué mano despertar?
¿con qué pie morir?
¿con qué ser pobre?
¿con qué voz callar?
¿con cuánto comprender, y luego, a quién?

No olvidar ni recordar
que por mucho cerrarla, robáronse la puerta,
y de sufrir tan poco estoy muy resentido,
y de tánto pensar, no tengo boca.

19 noviembre 1937

If it happened thus and thus putting it,
with what hand wake up?
with what foot die?
with what be poor?
with what voice quiet?
with how much understand, and then who?

Not to forget or remember
that by closing the door too often they stole it,
and from suffering too little I'm very resentful,
and from só much thinking, I've no mouth.

Al revés de las aves del monte,
que viven del valle,
aquí, una tarde,
aquí, presa, metaloso, terminante,
vino el Sincero con sus nietos pérfidos,
y nosotros quedámonos, que no hay
más madera en la cruz de la derecha,
ni más hierro en el clavo de la izquierda,
que un apretón de manos entre zurdos.

Vino el Sincero, ciego, con sus lámparas.
Se vió al Pálido, aquí, bastar
al Encarnado;
nació de puro humilde el Grande;
la guerra,
esta tórtola mía, nunca nuestra,
diseñóse, borróse, ovó, matáronla.

Llevóse el Ebrio al labio un roble, porque
amaba, y una astilla
de roble, porque odiaba;
trenzáronse las trenzas de los potros
y la crin de las potencias;
cantaron los obreros; fuí dichoso.

Contrary to those mountain birds
that live off the valley,
here one evening,
here, prey, metalish, final,
the Sincere came with his perfidious grandchildren,
and we stayed on, since there is no
more wood in the cross at the right
no more iron in the nail at the left
than a handclasp between lefthanded.

The Sincere came, blind with his lamps.
Here the Pale was seen, and was
for the Incarnate enough;
by sheer humbleness the Great was born;
the war,
this turtledove of mine, never ours,
sketched herself, effaced herself, laid eggs, they killed her.

The Intoxicated raised an oak to his lip because
he loved, and an oak
splinter because he hated;
the colts' braids were braided
and the mane of the powers;
the workers sang; I was happy.

El Pálido abrazóse al Encarnado
y el Ebrio, saludónos, escondiéndose.
Como era aquí y al terminar el día,
¡qué más tiempo que aquella plazoleta!
¡qué año mejor que esa gente!
¡qué momento más fuerte que ese siglo!

Pues de lo que hablo no es
sino de lo que pasa en esta época, y
de lo que ocurre en China y en España, y en el mundo.
(Walt Whitman tenía un pecho suavísimo y respiraba y nadie sabe lo que él hacía cuando
lloraba en su comedor.)

Pero, volviendo, a lo nuestro,
y al verso que decía, fuera entonces
que ví que el hombre es malnacido,
mal vivo, mal muerto, mal moribundo,
y, naturalmente,
el tartufo sincero desespérase,
el pálido (es el pálido de siempre)
será pálido por algo,
y el ebrio, entre la sangre humana y la leche animal,
abátese, da, y opta por marcharse.

Todo esto
agítase, ahora mismo,
en mi vientre de macho extrañamente.

20 noviembre 1937

The Pale hugged the Incarnate
and the Intoxicated, greeted us, hiding himself.
How it was here and when the day ended
what more time than that little square!
what better year than those people!
what moment stronger than that century!

For what I am talking about
is nothing else than what is happening today,
what is occurring in China and in Spain, and in the world.
(Walt Whitman had a very soft chest and breathed and no one
knows what he did when he cried in his dining room.)

But getting back, and to the question,
to the line I was speaking, it was then
I saw man is a son of a bitch born,
a son of a bitch alive, a son of a bitch
dead, a son of a bitch dying,
and, naturally,
the sincere tartuffe despairs,
the pale (pale as always)
will be for some reason pale,
and the intoxicated, between human blood and animal milk,
slumps, gives, and decides to take off.

All this
churns right now
in my male belly strangely.

Ello es que el lugar donde me pongo
el pantalón, es una casa donde
me quito la camisa en alta voz
y donde tengo un suelo, un alma, un mapa de mi España.
Ahora mismo hablaba
de mí conmigo, y ponía
sobre un pequeño libro un pan tremendo
y he, luego, hecho el traslado, he trasladado,
queriendo canturrear un poco, el lado
derecho de la vida al lado izquierdo;
más tarde, me he lavado todo, el vientre,
briosa dignamente;
he dado vuelta a ver lo que se ensucia,
he raspado lo que me lleva tan cerca
y he ordenado bien el mapa que
cabeceaba o lloraba, no lo sé.

Mi casa, por desgracia, es una casa,
un suelo por ventura, donde vive
con su inscripción mi cucharita amada,
mi querido esqueleto ya sin letras,
la navaja, un cigarro permanente.
De veras, cuando pienso
en lo que es la vida,
no puedo evitar de decírselo a Georgette,
a fin de comer algo agradable y salir,

The fact is the place where I put on my
pants is a house where
I take off my shirt out loud,
where I have floor, soul, a map of my Spain.
Just now I was talking about
me to myself, and put
on a little book a tremendous loaf of bread
and I've then made the move, I've moved,
trying to hum a little, the right
side of life to the left;
later, I've washed my whole body, my belly,
vigorously with dignity;
I've turned over to see what dirties itself,
I've scraped off what brings me so near
and put that map in proper order that
nodded off or wept, I don't know it.

My house, unfortunately, is a house,
a floor fortunately, where with its
inscription my beloved spoon lives,
my dear now letterless skeleton,
the razor, a permanent cigar.
Truthfully, when I think
what life is,
I can't help saying it to Georgette
so I can eat something pleasant and go out

por la tarde, comprar un buen periódico,
guardar un día para cuando no haya,
una noche también, para cuando haya
(así se dice en el Perú – me excuso);
del mismo modo, sufro con gran cuidado,
a fin de no gritar o de llorar, ya que los ojos
poseen, independientemente de uno, sus pobrezas,
quiero decir, su oficio, algo
que resbala del alma y cae al alma.

Habiendo atravesado
quince años; después, quince, y, antes, quince,
uno se siente, en realidad, tontillo,
es natural, por lo demás, ¡que hacer!
¡Y qué dejar de hacer, que es lo peor!
Sino vivir, sino llegar
á ser lo que es uno entre millones
de panes, entre miles de vinos, entre cientos de bocas,
entre el sol y su rayo que es de luna
y entre la misa, el pan, el vino y mi alma.

Hoy es domingo y, por eso,
me viene a la cabeza la idea, al pecho el llanto
y a la garganta, así como un gran bulto.
Hoy es domingo, y esto
tiene muchos siglos; de otra manera,
sería, quizá, lunes, y vendríame al corazón la idea,
al seso, el llanto
y a la garganta, una gana espantosa de ahogar
lo que ahora siento,
como un hombre que soy y que he sufrido.

21 noviembre 1937

for the evening, buy myself a good newspaper
and save a day for when there isn't one,
a night too, for when there is
(they put it this way in Peru – I'm sorry);
in the same way I suffer very carefully
so to not shout or cry, since the eyes
possess, independent of one, their poverties,
I mean, their duty, something
that slips away from the soul and falls to the soul.

Having crossed
fifteen years, after, fifteen, and before, fifteen,
one feels, actually, a little foolish,
it's natural, on the other hand, what to do!
And what not to do, that's worse!
Only to live, only to become
what one is among millions
of breads, among thousands of wines, among hundreds of mouths,
between the sun and its beam that's from the moon
and among the Mass, the bread, the wine and my soul.

Today is Sunday, and so
the idea comes to my head, to my chest the cry
and to my throat, like a big lump.
Today is Sunday, and this
is many centuries old; otherwise
it would be Monday maybe, the idea coming to my heart,
to my brain the cry
and to my throat a terrifying desire to choke
what I now feel,
like a man that I am and that I've suffered.

Algo te identifica con el que se aleja de ti, y es la facultad común de volver: de ahí tu más grande pesadumbre.

Algo te separa del que se queda contigo, y es la esclavitud común de partir: de ahí tus más nimios regocijos.

Me dirijo, en esta forma, a las individualidades colectivas, tanto como a las colectividades individuales y a los que, entre unas y otras, yacen marchando al son de las fronteras o, simplemente, marcan el paso inmóvil en el borde del mundo.

Algo típicamente neutro, de inexorablemente neutro, interpónese entre el ladrón y su víctima. Esto, asimismo, puede discernirse tratándose del cirujano y del paciente. Horrible medialuna, convexa y solar, cobija a unos y otros. Porque el objeto hurtado tiene también su peso indiferente, y el órgano intervenido, también su grasa triste.

¿Qué hay de más desesperante en la tierra, que la imposibilidad en que se halla el hombre feliz de ser infortunado y el hombre bueno de ser malvado?

¡Alejarse! ¡Quedarse! ¡Volver! ¡Partir! Toda la mecánica social cabe en estas palabras.

24 noviembre 1937

Something identifies you with the one who pulls away from you, and it's the common faculty of returning: thus your overwhelming grief.

Something separates you from the one who stays with you, and it's the common slavery of parting: thus your puny rejoicing.

In this way I address myself to collective individualities as well as to individual collectivities and to those who, between some and others, lie buried marching to the sound of the frontiers or simply mark motionless time at world's edge.

Something typically neuter, of inexorable neuterness, thrusts itself between the thief and his victim. At the same time such can be discerned regarding the surgeon and his patient. Horrible convex and solar half-moon covers some and others. For the robbed object has its indifferent weight too, and the probed organ likewise its sad fat.

What on earth is more desperate than the impossible situation in which the happy man finds himself when he is unfortunate and in which the good man finds himself when he is wicked?

To pull away! To stay! To return! To part! The whole social mechanism fits in these words.

En suma, no poseo para expresar mi vida sino mi muerte. Y, después de todo, al cabo de la escalonada naturaleza y del gorrión en bloque, me duermo, mano a mano con mi sombra.

Y, al descender del acto venerable y del otro gemido, me reposo pensando en la marcha impertérrita del tiempo.

¿Por qué la cuerda, entonces, si el aire es tan sencillo? ¿Para qué la cadena, si existe el hierro por sí sólo?

César Vallejo, el acento con que amas, el verbo con que escribes, el vientecillo con que oyes, sólo saben de ti por tu garganta.

César Vallejo, póstrate, por eso, con indistinto orgullo, con tálamo de ornamentales áspides y exagonales ecos.

Restitúyete al corpóreo panal, a la beldad; aroma los florecidos corchos, cierra ambas grutas al sañudo antropoide; repara, en fin, tu antipático venado; tente pena.

¡Que no hay cosa más densa que el odio en voz pasiva, ni más mísera ubre que el amor!

¡Que ya no puedo andar, sino en dos harpas!

¡Que ya no me conoces, sino porque te sigo instrumental, prolijamente!

¡Que ya no doy gusanos, sino breves!

¡Que ya te implico tanto, que medio que te afilas!

¡Que ya llevo unas tímidas legumbres y otras bravas!
Pues el afecto que quiébrase de noche en mis bronquios, lo trajeron de día ocultos deanes y, si amanezco pálido, es por mi obra; y si anochezco rojo, por mi obrero. Ello explica,

In sum, to express my life I have only my death. And after everything that's happened, at the end of scaled nature and of the massed sparrow, I fall asleep hand to hand with my shadow.

And on descending from the venerable act and from the other groan, I repose thinking about the intrepid march of time.

Why the rope, then, if air's so simple? What's the chain for, if iron exists by itself?

César Vallejo, the accent with which you love, the word with which you write, the little wind with which you hear, only know of you by your throat.

César Vallejo, prostrate yourself for that, with indistinct pride, with a nuptial couch of ornamental asps and hexagonal echoes.

Give yourself back to the corporeal honeycomb, to Beauty; aroma the flowered corks, shut both grots to the enraged anthropoid; in short, mend your disagreeable stag; grieve for yourself.

For there's nothing denser than hate in the passive voice, no stingier udder than love!

For I can't walk any longer except in two harps!

For you no longer know me, for instrumental, longwindedly, I hound you!

For I no longer bear worms, I bear closed vowels!

igualmente, estos cansancios y estos despojos, mis famosos tíos. Ello explica, en fin, esta lágrima que brindo por la dicha de los hombres.

¡César Vallejo, parece
mentira que así tarden tus parientes,
sabiendo que ando cautivo,
sabiendo que yaces libre!
¡Vistosa y perra suerte!
¡César Vallejo, te odio con ternura!

26 noviembre 1937

For now I implicate you so much you nearly whet to nothing!

For now I carry not only timid but ferocious vegetables! Thus the love that ruptures during the night in my bronchia, secret deans brought during the day and, if I wake pale, it's because of my work; and if I sunset red, because of my worker. This explains equally these fatigues and this refuse, my famed uncles. This explains, in short, this tear I toast for the happiness of men.

César Vallejo, it's simply
incredible that your relatives linger like this,
knowing that I go chained,
knowing that you rest freed!
Fit to kill luck of a dog!
César Vallejo, I hate you with tenderness!

Otro poco de calma, camarada;
un mucho inmenso, septentrional, completo,
feroz, de calma chica,
al servicio menor de cada triunfo
y en la audaz servidumbre del fracaso.

Embriaguez te sobra, y no hay
tanta locura en la razón, como este
tu raciocinio muscular, y no hay
más racional error que tu experiencia.

Pero, hablando más claro
y pensándolo en oro, eres de acero,
a condición que no seas
tonto y rehuses
entusiasmarte por la muerte tánto
y por la vida, con tu sola tumba.

Necesario es que sepas
contener tu volumen sin correr, sin afligirte,
tu realidad molecular entera
y más allá, la marcha de tus vivas
y más acá, tus mueras legendarios.

¡Eres de acero, como dicen,
con tal que no tiembles y no vayas

Another touch of calm, comrade;
an immense northern complete ferocious
much of small calm,
in less service each triumph
facing the daring servitude of the disaster.

You've highs to spare, and there's not
so much madness in the mind, as in this
your muscular reasoning, and there's no
more rational error than your experience.

But, speaking more clear
and thinking it in gold, you are steel
on condition you are not
stupid and refuse to
delight because of death truly
and because of life, in your one tomb.

You must learn to
contain your volume without running, without hanging yourself up,
your entire molecular reality—
and beyond that, the march of your "vivas"
and closer home, your legendary "down withs."

You are steel, as they say,
providing you don't tremble and don't

a reventar, compadre
de mi cálculo, enfático ahijado
de mis sales luminosas!

Anda, no más; resuelve,
considera tu crisis, suma, sigue,
tájala, bájala, ájala;
el destino, las energías íntimas, los catorce
versículos del pan; ¡cuántos diplomas
y poderes, al borde fehaciente de tu arranque!
¡Cuánto detalle en síntesis, contigo!
¡Cuánta presión idéntica, a tus pies!
¡Cuánto rigor y cuánto patrocinio!

Es idiota
ese método de padecimiento,
esa luz modulada y virulenta,
si con sólo la calma haces señales
serias, características fatales.

Vamos a ver, hombre;
cuéntame lo que me pasa,
que yo, aunque grite, estoy siempre a tus órdenes.

28 noviembre 1937

explode, godbrother
of my calculation, emphatic godson
of my luminous salts!

Go right ahead; solve,
consider your crisis, add, carry,
trim it, diminish it, crumple it up;
destiny, the intimate energies, the fourteen
versicles of bread; how many diplomas
and powers at the authentic brink of your start!
How múch detail in synthesis with you!
How múch identical pressure at your feet!
How múch rigidity and how much patronage!

It's idiotic
that method of enduring,
that modulated virulent light,
if with only the calm you flash serious
signs, fatal characteristics.

Let's see, man;
let me know what's happening to me,
for I'm always, even though I shout, at your command.

Los Desgraciados

Ya va a venir el día; da
cuerda a tu brazo, búscate debajo
del colchón, vuelve a pararte
en tu cabeza, para andar derecho.
Ya va a venir el día, ponte el saco.

Ya va a venir el día; ten
fuerte en la mano a tu intestino grande, reflexiona,
antes de meditar, pues es horrible
cuando le cae a uno la desgracia
y se le cae a uno a fondo el diente.

Necesitas comer, pero, me digo,
no tengas pena, que no es de pobres
la pena, el sollozar junto a su tumba;
remiéndate, recuerda,
confía en tu hilo blanco, fuma, pasa lista
a tu cadena y guárdala detrás de tu retrato.
Ya va a venir el día, ponte el alma.

Ya va a venir el día; pasan,
han abierto en el hotel un ojo,
azotándolo, dándole con un espejo tuyo . . .
¿tiemblas? Es el estado remoto de la frente
y la nación reciente del estómago.
Roncan aún . . . ¡Qué universo se lleva este ronquido!

The Wretched of the Earth

The day's going to come; wind
up your arm, look under
your mattress, stand again
on your head to walk straight.
The day's going to come, put on your coat.

The day's going to come; grip
your large intestine tight in your hand, reflect
before you meditate, for it's awful
when your wretchedness hits and sinks
on and on in you a tooth.

You have to eat, but I keep telling myself
don't grieve, for grief and graveside
sobbing don't belong to the poor;
pull yourself together, remember,
confide in your white thread, smoke, check
your chain and keep it behind your portrait.
The day's going to come, put on your soul.

The day's going to come; they pass,
they've opened up an eye in the hotel
whipping and beating it with a mirror that's yours . . .
are you trembling? It's the remote state of the forehead
and this recent nation of the stomach.
They're still snoring . . . What universe puts up with this
snore!

¡Cómo quedan tus poros, enjuiciándolo!
¡Con cuántos doses, ¡ay! estás tan solo!
Ya va a venir el día, ponte el sueño.

Ya va a venir el día, repito
por el órgano oral de tu silencio
y urge tomar la izquierda con el hambre
y tomar la derecha con la sed; de todos modos,
abstente de ser pobre con los ricos,
atiza
tu frío, porque en él se integra mi calor, amada víctima.
Ya va a venir el día, ponte el cuerpo.

Ya va a venir el día;
la mañana, la mar, el meteoro, van
en pos de tu cansancio, con banderas,
y, por tu orgullo clásico, las hienas
cuentan sus pasos al compás del asno,
la panadera piensa en ti,
el carnicero piensa en ti, palpando
el hacha en que están presos
el acero y el hierro y el metal; jamás olvides
que durante la misa no hay amigos.
Ya va a venir el día, ponte el sol.

Ya viene el día; dobla
el aliento, triplica
tu bondad rencorosa
y da codos al miedo, nexo y énfasis,
pues tú, como se observa en tu entrepierna y siendo
el malo, ¡ay! inmortal,
has soñado esta noche que vivías
de nada y morías de todo . . .

[*Fin de noviembre o primera semana de diciembre 1937.*]

How your pores hang on, indicting it!
With so many twos, ay! you're so alone!
The day's going to come, put on your dream.

The day's going to come, I repeat
through the oral organ of your silence
and urge you to move further left with hunger
further right with thirst; in any case
stop being poor with the rich,
poker
your cold, for in it is mixed my warmth, beloved victim.
The day's going to come, put on your body.

The day's going to come;
morning, sea, meteor
pursue your weariness with banners,
and through your classic pride, the hyenas
count their steps to the beat of the ass,
the baker's wife thinks about you,
the butcher thinks about you, fingering
the cleaver in which steel
iron and metal are imprisoned; never forget
that during Mass there are no friends.
The day's going to come, put on your sun.

The day comes; double
your breathing, triple
your rancorous goodwill
and elbow fear, link and emphasis,
for you, as anyone can see in your crotch the evil
being, ay! immortal,
you've dreamed tonight you were living
on nothing and dying from everything . . .

[*End of November or the first week of December, 1937.*]

Sermón Sobre la Muerte

Y, en fin, pasando luego al dominio de la muerte,
que actúa en escuadrón, previo corchete,
párrafo y llave, mano grande y diéresis,
¿a qué el pupitre asirio? ¿a qué el cristiano púlpito,
el intenso jalón del mueble vándalo
o, todavía menos, este esdrújulo retiro?

¿Es para terminar,
mañana, en prototipo del alarde fálico,
en diabetes y en blanca vacinica,
en rostro geométrico, en difunto,
que se hacen menester sermón y almendras,
que sobran literalmente patatas
y este espectro fluvial en que arde el oro
y en que se quema el precio de la nieve?
¿Es para eso, que morimos tánto?
¿Para sólo morir,
tenemos que morir, a cada instante?
¿Y el párrafo que escribo?
¿Y el corchete deísta que enarbolo?
¿Y el escuadrón en que falló mi casco?
¿Y la llave que va a todas las puertas?
¿Y la forense diéresis, la mano,
mi patata y mi carne y mi contradicción bajo la sábana?

¡Loco de mí, lobo de mí, cordero
de mí, sensato, caballísimo de mí!

Sermon on Death

And, finally, passing then into the domain of death
that drills in squadron, former bracket,
paragraph and brace, pieced brace and dieresis,
for what the Assyrian podium? for what the Christian pulpit?
the intense landmark of the Vandal furniture
or even less this proparoxytonic retreat?

Is it in order to end
tomorrow in prototype of the phallic show,
in diabetes and in white bedpan,
in geometric face and in defunct,
that sermon and almonds are made fundamental,
that there are literally too many potatoes
and this watery specter in which gold burns
and in which the price of snow scalds?
Is it for this we die so much?
Only to die
must we die each instant?
And the paragraph I write?
And the deistic bracket I raise on high?
And the squadron in which my hoof is failed?
And the brace that fits all doors?
And the stranger dieresis, the hand,
my potato and my flesh and my contradiction under the sheet?

Weird weird me, werewolf of me, lamb-
heart, judicious stallion, O great workhorse of me!

¡Pupitre, sí, toda la vida; púlpito,
también, toda la muerte!
Sermón de la barbarie: estos papeles;
esdrújulo retiro: este pellejo.

De esta suerte, cogitabundo, aurífero, brazudo,
defenderé mi presa en dos momentos,
con la voz y también con la laringe,
y del olfato físico con que oro
y del instinto de inmovilidad con que ando,
me honraré mientras viva – hay que decirlo;
se enorgullecerán mis moscardones,
porque, al centro, estoy yo, y a la derecha,
también, y, a la izquierda, de igual modo.

8 diciembre 1937

Podium, yes, my whole life; pulpit
likewise, my whole death!
These papers a barbaric sermon;
proparoxytonic retreat of this peelable skin.

Of this luck, thoughtful, auriferous, flank-armed,
I'll defend my catch in two moments
with voice and likewise with larynx,
and of the physical smell with which I pray,
and of the instinct for immobility with which I walk,
I shall honor myself while I live – it must be said;
my botflies will swell with pride,
because, at the center, I exist, and to the right
likewise, and, to the left, equally.

Cualquiera que sea la causa que tenga que defender ante Dios,
más allá de la muerte, tengo un defensor: Dios.

Whatever may be the cause I have to defend
before God, beyond death I have a defender: God.